SUMMER BRIDGE LEARNING FOR MINECRAFTERS

Bridging Grades 1-2

by Nancy Rogers Bosse

Illustrated by Amanda Brack

Sky Pony Press
New York

Sky Pony Press books may be purchased in bulk at special discounts for sales promotion, corporate gifts, fund-raising, or educational purposes. Special editions can also be created to specifications. For details, contact the Special Sales Department, Sky Pony Press, 307 West 36th Street, 11th Floor, New York, NY 10018 or info@skyhorsepublishing.com.

Sky Pony® is a registered trademark of Skyhorse Publishing, Inc.®, a Delaware corporation.

Minecraft® is a registered trademark of Notch Development AB.
The Minecraft game is copyright © Mojang AB.

Visit our website at www.skyponypress.com.

Authors, books, and more at SkyPonyPressBlog.com.

10 9 8 7 6 5 4 3 2 1

Cover art by Bill Greenhead
Cover design by Brian Peterson

Interior art by Amanda Brack

All other art used with permission from Shutterstock.com

Print ISBN: 978-1-5107-3597-2

Printed in China

A NOTE TO PARENTS

You probably know the importance of having your child practice the key skills taught in the classroom. And you are probably hoping that your kid will be on board with practicing at home. Well, congratulations! You've come to the right place! *The Summer Bridge Learning for Minecrafters, Bridging Grades 1 – 2* transforms learning into an adventure complete with zombies, skeletons, and creepers.

You will love that *Summer Bridge Learning for Minecrafters, Bridging Grades 1 – 2* aligns with the National Core Standards for math and English language arts (ELA), as well as national, state, and district recommendations for science and social studies. Every page reinforces a key concept in one of the subject areas. Your child will love the colorful art, familiar video game characters, and the fun approach to each learning activity!

The pages of this workbook are color coded to help you target specific skills areas as needed.

BLUE	Language Arts
ORANGE	Math
GREEN	Science
PINK	Social Studies

Whether it's the joy of seeing their favorite Minecrafting characters on every page, the fun of solving a riddle or a puzzle, or the pride of accomplishment of completing a learning challenge, there is something in this book for even the most reluctant learner.

Happy adventuring!

CONTENTS

LONG OR SHORT VOWEL SOUND

Read each word. Listen for the vowel sound. Circle long or short.

1. grass	2. clay	3. bat
long short	long short	long short
4. fish	**5. bone**	**6. wheat**
long short	long short	long short
7. chest	**8. map**	**9. ice**
long short	long short	long short

LONG OR SHORT VOWEL SOUND

Read each word. Listen for the vowel sound. Circle long or short.

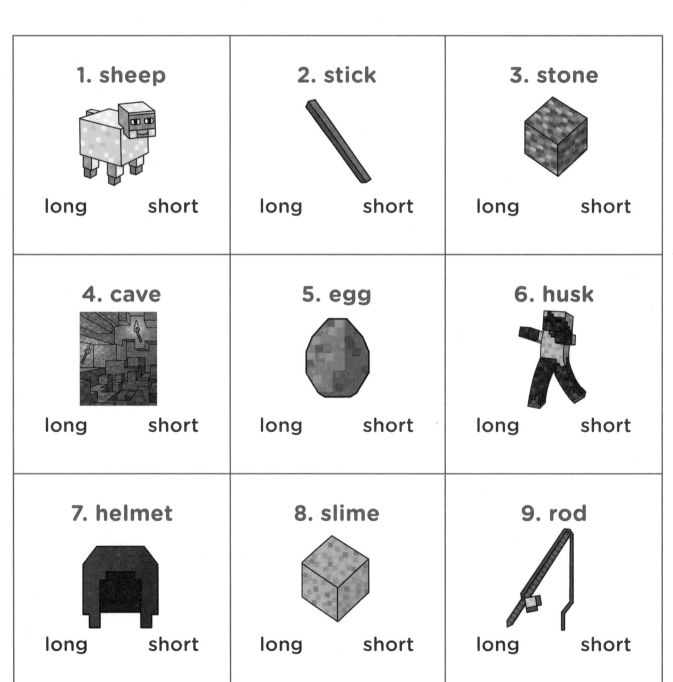

1. sheep

long   short

2. stick

long   short

3. stone

long   short

4. cave

long   short

5. egg

long   short

6. husk

long   short

7. helmet

long   short

8. slime

long   short

9. rod

long   short

SHORT VOWEL WORDS

Read each word and notice its short vowel sound.
Draw a line to match the word to the picture.

1. cat

A.

2. block

B.

3. squid

C.

4. hug

D.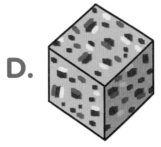

5. gems

E.

SHORT VOWEL WORDS

Read each sentence. Listen for the short vowel sounds. Draw a picture to match the sentence.

The witch has a hat.

The villager has emeralds.

The dog's collar is red.

The cat wants some fish.

DIGRAPHS

Two consonants that stand together in a word and make one sound are called **digraphs**. Ch, th, and sh are digraphs. Write the correct digraph under the picture.

1.	**2.**	**3.**
_____ read	_____ eep	_____ icken
4.	**5.**	**6.**
_____ est	_____ ield	_____ ears
7.	**8.**	**9.**
_____ istle	_____ eese	_____ ief

R-CONTROLLED VOWELS

The sound of a vowel changes when the vowel is followed by an 'r.' The words below have r-controlled vowels. Draw a line to connect each word to its picture.

1. torch

A.

2. star

B.

3. church

C.

4. horse

D.

5. dirt

E.

6. sword

F.

LONG VOWELS SILENT-E

RACE
The e at the end of a word makes the vowel long.

Write the word that names each picture.
Write one letter in each block.

blaze   rose   cake   slime   cube

1.

2.

3.

4.

5.

When two vowels are together in a word, the first is long and the second is silent.

LONG VOWELS

Write the word for each picture. Underline the vowel team that makes the long vowel sound.

| meat | pie | blue | tail | beet | goat |

1. _____

2. _____

3. _____

4. _____

5. _____

6. _____

LONG VOWELS

Write ow, ay, or igh to spell each word.

Sometimes, ow says long o, ay says long a, and igh says long i.

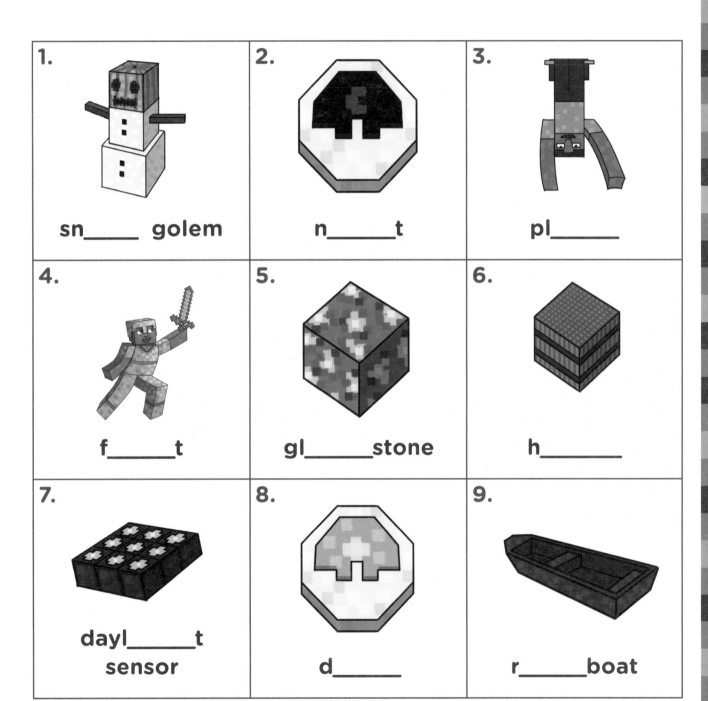

1. sn_____ golem

2. n_____t

3. pl_____

4. f_____t

5. gl_____stone

6. h_____

7. dayl_____t sensor

8. d_____

9. r_____boat

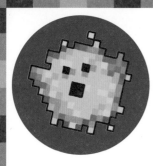

LONG VOWELS

Complete the crossword puzzle with long vowel words.

rain	creeper	wheat
blaze	Steve	mule
hay	night	snow

boat	pie
cube	ate

Across

1 a mob that explodes

4 food for horses

6 a flaming, hostile mob

7 used to make snow golems

9 cows and sheep will eat this

10 an offspring of a horse and a donkey

11 used to travel on water

Down

1 the shape of a block

2 a dessert made with pumpkin

3 water that falls from the sky

5 past tense of eat

7 an avatar, like Alex

8 opposite of day

PREFIXES

Prefixes can be added before a word to change its meaning.

re means again → **re**view means to view again
un means not → **un**seen means not seen
pre means before → **pre**view means to view before

Underline the prefix. Draw a line to connect the word to its meaning.

1. replay

2. unopened

3. premix

4. retry

5. unhappy

A. to mix before

B. not happy

C. not opened

D. to play again

E. to try again

I should be called an exploder!

SUFFIXES

Suffixes can be added at the end of a word to change its meaning.

er means one who does → farm**er** means one who farms
ful means full of → help**ful** means full of help
less means without → care**less** means without care

Underline the suffix. Draw a line to connect the word to its meaning.

1. fearless

2. villager

3. joyful

4. creeper

5. fearful

A. full of fear

B. full of joy

C. one who lives in a village

D. without fear

E. one who creeps

COMPOUND WORDS

Read each compound word. Draw a line between the two words. Number one has been done for you.

Compound words are made up of two words, like Enderman.

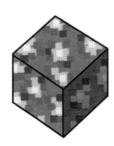 1. pork|chop	 2. pufferfish	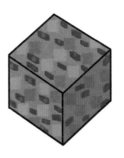 3. redstone
 4. beetroot	 5. chestplate	 6. swampland
 7. pickaxe	 8. glowstone	 9. fireball

COMPOUND WORDS

Combine two words to write a compound word that matches each picture.

Hint: One of the words in the box is used twice.

man	door	drum	silver	pig
stick	knob	fish	ender	

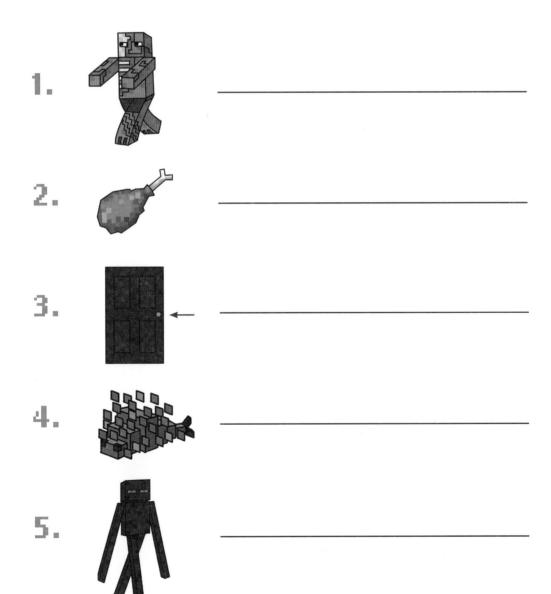

1. _____

2. _____

3. ← _____

4. _____

5. _____

SYLLABLES

Say the word. Write the number of syllables on the line.

Hint: A syllable is a part of a word. Every syllable has a vowel sound.

 pig has
one syllable

 pigman has
two syllables

1. cow ....

5. fish ....

2. chicken ....

6. skeleton ....

3. ghast ....

7. villager ....

4. witch ....

8. Ender
dragon ....

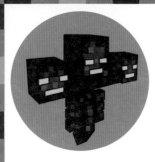

DIVIDING SYLLABLES

Draw a line between the syllables of each word.
The first one is done for you.

Hints:
- Every syllable has a vowel sound.
- Sometimes words divide between two consonants.
- Never divide between the two letters of a digraph like sh, th, or ch.

1. mush|room

2. compass

3. cactus

4. rabbit

5. saddle

6. banner

7. wither

8. anvil

WHAT DOES IT MEAN?

Read each sentence. Use the context to figure out the meaning of the bolded word. Then circle the best meaning.

Hint: Sometimes clues to a word's meaning can be found in the picture.

1. The **guardian** protects the temple.

   one who hurts   **or**   one who takes care of

2. The gold **ingots** are stacked up high.

   balls   **or**   blocks

3. Steve **crafted** a diamond sword with two diamonds and a stick.

   found   **or**   made

4. The player **stashes** gems in a chest for safe keeping.

   hides away   **or**   shows

ALL ABOUT ENDERMEN

Read about Endermen. Use context clues to figure out the meaning of the bolded words. Circle the best meaning.

The Enderman can be found in the End or the Overworld. It has long **limbs** and purple eyes. If you stare into its eyes, you will die. It will not attack unless **provoked** or annoyed. The Enderman's **invisibility** keeps it from being seen. When damaged, the Enderman will **teleport**, moving instantly to a new place far away.

1. Overworld means:
a world above ground   **OR**   a world under ground

2. limbs means:
head and neck   **OR**   arms and legs

3. provoked means:
loved   **OR**   bothered

4. invisibility means:
able to be seen   **OR**   not able to be seen

5. teleport means:
to stay in one place   **OR**   to move away

SUBJECT AND VERB

Circle the correct verb in each sentence.
Then draw a line to the correct picture.

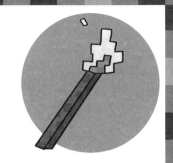

1. The creeper explode / explodes.

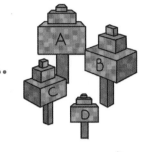

A.

2. Alex run / runs fast.

B.

3. The trees grow / grows.

C.

4. The Ender Dragon fly / flies.

D.

5. The squids swim / swims.

E.

VERB TENSE

*Read each sentence. Add **ing** or **ed** to make each underlined verb correct.*

1. Alex <u>is play</u>_____ with the farm animals.

2. The librarian <u>help</u>_____ Steve find a book.

3. The zombies <u>attack</u>_____ the villagers.

4. The zombie <u>is fall</u>_____ into the lava.

5. Steve <u>is craft</u>_____ a diamond sword.

PLURAL NOUNS

Write the plural of each word.

Plural means more than one. Add *s* to make most nouns plural.

- Add an 's' to the end to make most words plural.
- When a word ends in *o, s, x, ch, sh,* or *th*, add es.
- When a word ends in consonant-y, change y to i and add es.
- When a word ends in f, change the f to v and add es.

1. wolf  _____

2. poppy  _____

3. church  _____

4. husk  _____

5. day  _____

ADJECTIVES

Choose an adjective to finish each sentence. Then underline the word the adjective describes.

| pink | fast | tall | hungry | scary |

1. Alex is _____.

2. The _____ pig lives on the farm.

3. The _____ horse ate the carrot.

4. The haunted house looks _____.

5. The Enderman is _____.

CONJUNCTIONS

Write the conjunction that best completes the sentence.

and   **or**   **but**   **so**

1. Steve waters the plants _____ they will grow.

2. Is Steve reading a book _____ doing math?

3. Steve loves cake, _____ he will eat it.

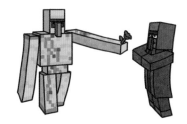

4. Iron golems give poppies to villagers, _____ not to other iron golems.

5. Steve _____ Alex are laughing.

PREPOSITIONS

Look at the picture. Write a preposition that best completes the sentence.

Prepositions tell position.

by
on
under
in

1. The kid with the green shoes is _____ the slide tunnel.

2. The boy with the ball is _____ the blacktop.

3. The boy in the orange shirt is _____ the rings.

4. The girl in the pink shirt is _____ the swing.

5. The girl in the green shirt is sitting _____ the blacktop.

FIX THE SENTENCE

Copy the sentence. Fix the errors.

Sentences start with a capital letter and end with a period or question mark.

1. have you seen a shulker

_____

2. a shulker is a hostile mob

_____

3. it hides in its shell

_____

4. its shell looks like a purpur block

_____

5. it opens its shell to peek outside

_____

WRITING SENTENCES

Sentences start with a capital letter and end with a period.

Rearrange the words to write a sentence.

1. is diamond   Steve   wearing   armor

_____

2. like creepers explode to

_____

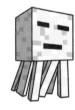

3. in   ghasts   Nether   live   the

_____

4. for   villagers   watch   zombie   out

_____

SENTENCES

Read each sentence. Write **C**, if the sentence is complete. Write **I**, if the sentence is incomplete.

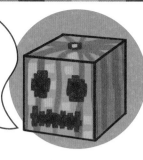
A sentence is a complete thought. It needs a subject (who or what) and a verb (the action).

 **1.** The rabbit hops.

 2. The shulker in a shell.

 **3.** The silverfish with gray scales.

 4. The horse eats a carrot.

 **5.** The eye of Ender.

COMPLETE THE SENTENCE

Choose the phrase that will make a complete sentence and write it on the line. Add a period.

1. A zombie _____

rides a chicken   and a chicken

2. Baby zombies _____

with armor   **do not burn in sunlight**

3. Husks _____

spawn from zombies   and zombies with golden swords

4. A zombie _____

with full golden armor   **attacked**

ADDING DETAILS

Rewrite the sentence adding details to make the sentence more interesting.

Adjectives (describe people and things)		**Adverbs** (describe actions)	
dangerous	poisonous	viciously	quickly
small	angry	creepily	awkwardly
wicked	giant	angrily	suddenly

1. The _____ evoker _____
               adjective   adverb
used the fang attack.

2. The _____ silverfish spawned _____
              adjective   adverb
from a monster egg.

3. The _____ zombie _____
               adjective   adverb
rode a chicken.

4. Endermen _____ attacked the
                             adverb
_____ endermite.
               adjective

ADDING DETAILS

Add details to the sentences to tell how, when, and where. Use words from the box or your own words.

how	when	where
quickly	yesterday	in the jungle
bravely	after dinner	to his house
happily	before breakfast	on the farm
angrily	during the night	in the End

1. Steve ran.

Steve ran quickly during the night to his house.

2. Alex played.

_____

_____

3. The creeper exploded.

_____

_____

4. The mooshroom walked.

_____

_____

WRITING SENTENCES

Write a detailed sentence to tell about each picture.
Use the words in the word boxes to help you.

Nouns		Verbs	
iron golem	gold	wore	wanted
baby	armor	told	ate
zombie	horse	marched	cried
poppy	carrot	gave	fought

1. _____

_____

2. _____

_____

3. _____

_____

4. _____

_____

WRITING SENTENCES

Write what you think is happening in the image below.

_____

_____

_____

_____

_____

_____

FACT OR OPINION

A fact is something that can be proven true or false. An opinion is a feeling about something.

*Circle **F** if the sentence is a fact.*
*Circle **O** if the sentence is an opinion.*

1. A mooshroom looks like a cow.   F   O

2. A mooshroom is better than a cow.   F   O

3. Alex is the coolest avatar.   F   O

4. Alex ran away from the zombies.   F   O

5. The wolf is my favorite.   F   O

6. The wolf can be tamed.   F   O

7. The squid is a character in the game.   F   O

8. The squid is black.   F   O

IN MY OPINION

Who's the better mob – iron golem, creeper, or skeleton? Fill in the blanks to write your opinion. Give three reasons for your opinion.

In my opinion, _____ is the
write the name of the mob

best mob. One reason is _____

_____

Another reason is _____

_____

The last reason is _____

_____

That is why _____ is the
write the name of the mob

best mob.

WRITE A STORY

Use the characters and setting pictured to write a story.

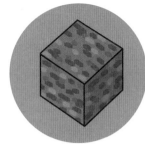

characters

villager   zombie   witch

setting

village

_____

_____

_____

_____

_____

_____

SEQUENCING

Read about how to tame a horse. Then number the steps in the correct order.

How to Tame a Horse

An apple will instantly tame a horse. But if you don't have an apple, taming a horse will be difficult. First, feed the horse to calm its temper. A horse cannot be tamed until its temper fades. Next, put its saddle on its back. A horse must be ridden to be tamed. Continue feeding the horse as you ride it. Finally, you will have a tame horse.

_____ The horse is tamed.

_____ Feed the horse.

_____ Continue to feed the horse.

_____ Ride the horse.

_____ Put a saddle on the horse.

SEQUENCING

Read about how to craft a diamond sword.
Then number the steps in the correct order.

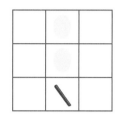

How to Craft a Diamond Sword

A diamond sword is a good weapon to have. It can do the most damage. To craft a diamond sword, you will need two diamonds and a stick. Open your crafting table. Place the first diamond in the middle box in the first row. Then place the second diamond in the middle box of the second row. Finally, place the stick in the middle box of the third row.

_____ **Place the second diamond in the middle box of the second row.**

_____ **Collect two diamonds and a stick.**

_____ **Place the stick in the middle box of the third row.**

_____ **Open the crafting table.**

_____ **Place the first diamond in the middle box of the first row.**

LOGICAL THINKING

When mobs are destroyed, they drop an item. Read the clues to determine which item each mob drops.

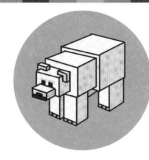

Hint: Put an X in the box when you know the item is not dropped by a mob.

Put an O in the box when you know a mob drops that item.

Iron golem drops something living.

 Cow does not drop something that swims.

Chicken drops something that is part of its body.

 Polar bear drops something it eats.

	fish	feather	leather	poppy
cow				
chicken				
polar bear				
iron golem				

IT'S IN THE DETAILS

Draw a picture to tell a story about a make-believe place like the End. Include lots of details in your picture. Then write a story about your picture on the next page.

COMPARE AND CONTRAST

Read about zombies and skeletons. Then, use the Venn diagram to compare and contrast them.

Zombies and Skeletons

Zombies and skeletons are hostile mobs. They are undead. They burn in the sun. Skeletons run away when attacked. Zombies fight back. Skeletons climb ladders. Zombies stay away from tall cliffs. When killed, zombies drop rotten flesh, but skeletons drop bones.

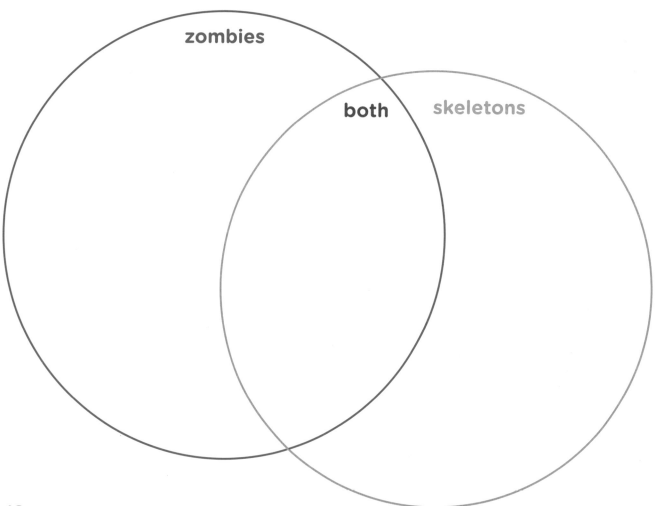

zombies

both   skeletons

SKIP COUNTING

Skip count to answer each question.

1. Skip count by 2s to count the skeleton legs.

_____ _____ _____ _____ _____ _____ _____

_____ _____ _____ _____ _____ _____ _____

How many legs in all? _____

2. Skip count by 5s to count the blocks in the towers.

_____ _____ _____ _____ _____ _____ _____ _____ _____ _____

How many blocks in all? _____

I'll trade you some of my redstone for emeralds.

SKIP COUNTING

Skip count by 10s to count the rows of redstone blocks. Write the numbers on each line.

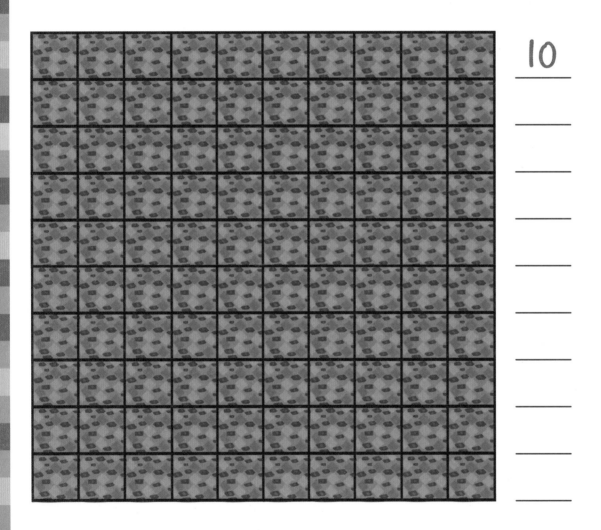

10

_____

_____

_____

_____

_____

_____

_____

_____

How many blocks in all? _____

EVEN OR ODD

Color the numbers to reveal a valuable weapon.

- ■ odd numbers to 20
- ■ odd number 21 - 100
- ■ even numbers 21 – 100
- ■ even numbers to 20

22	46	74	26	62	34	52	94	28	34	72	30	3	11	9
62	94	40	64	76	64	26	30	96	48	32	19	25	73	17
54	92	84	38	28	76	50	76	98	100	13	39	57	61	7
48	36	66	24	30	50	74	98	66	15	33	27	43	3	70
70	38	74	58	78	36	100	80	7	43	35	81	5	34	92
82	46	7	13	26	56	54	15	51	31	47	17	60	82	68
90	68	11	2	3	78	11	37	21	75	5	46	54	32	84
88	24	60	9	16	7	99	41	93	15	94	96	24	36	58
44	80	28	17	12	15	23	87	13	46	66	24	52	68	100
26	38	62	90	9	6	9	17	70	64	88	86	74	22	98
64	40	86	5	14	7	8	16	11	22	60	58	66	36	68
28	100	17	18	13	42	15	13	10	5	42	24	44	88	56
15	7	20	5	48	36	52	60	7	3	36	56	38	62	90
11	4	13	30	68	50	62	74	24	56	42	38	76	88	72
19	3	17	44	52	64	82	58	22	54	32	32	54	100	40

PATTERNS

Look at the set of numbers and find the pattern. Draw a line between the numbers and the pattern. Complete the pattern.

1. 2, 4, 6, 8, _____ , _____ , _____   A. + 10

2. 55, 50, 45, 40, _____ , _____ , _____   B. + 5

3. 40, 50, 60, 70, _____ , _____ , _____   C. + 2

4. 12, 10, 8, 6, _____ , _____ , _____   D. + 3

5. 60, 65, 70, 75, _____ , _____ , _____   E. - 2

6. 9, 12, 15, 18, _____ , _____ , _____   F. - 5

ADD TO 20

Draw each problem using lines for tens and dots for ones. Then count and add. The first one is done for you.

| = 10 ● = 1

1.

13
+ 4
———
17

| ● ● ●
● ● ● ●

2.

16
+ 3
———

3.

12
+ 7
———

4.

14
+ 3
———

5.

13
+ 3
———

6.

15
+ 3
———

ADD TO 20

Solve each problem. Use the answers to solve the riddle.

Question: Why is the witch bad at math?

1. 11 + 7 ——— O	**2.** 15 + 2 ——— T	**3.** 13 + 6 ——— L	**4.** 12 + 3 ——— N
5. 5 + 6 ——— E	**6.** 12 + 1 ——— I	**7.** 8 + 6 ——— S	**8.** 7 + 5 ——— Y
9. 13 + 3 ——— A	**10.** 3 + 7 ——— P	**11.** 6 + 2 ——— D	**12.** 16 + 4 ——— R

Answer: _____ _____   _____ _____ _____ _____
     13   17   18   15   19   12

_____ _____ _____ _____ _____ _____   _____ _____
  19   11   16   20   15   11   8   17   18

_____ _____ _____ _____ _____ .
  14   10   11   19   19

SUBTRACT WITHIN 20

Draw lines and dots to show the first number.
Then cross out the second number.
Count the amount that's left. The first
one is done for you.

| = 10   ● = 1

1.

17 | ●●●●●●●
- 6

||

2.

19
- 7

3.

18
- 5

4.

17
- 3

5.

16
-10

6.

15
- 12

SUBTRACT WITHIN 20

Solve each problem. Use the answers to solve the riddle.

Question: How did the villager learn to subtract?

1. 11 − 3 _____ I	**2.** 16 − 7 _____ K	**3.** 19 − 7 _____ A	**4.** 17 − 4 _____ U
5. 19 − 12 _____ T	**6.** 13 − 9 _____ O	**7.** 15 − 5 _____ L	**8.** 17 − 6 _____ M
9. 18 − 4 _____ B	**10.** 17 − 14 _____ C	**11.** 19 − 14 _____ F	**12.** 15 − 9 _____ D

Answer: ___ ___ ___ ___ ___ ___ ___
      12   14 8   7   4   5

___ ___ ___ ___   ___ ___ ___ ___
6 13 11 14   10 13 3 9

WHAT'S MISSING?

Fill in the missing number in each table.

1.

♥♥♥♥♥♥♥♥♥♥ ♥♥♥♥♥♥♥♥♥	
19	
8	

2.

♥♥♥♥♥♥♥♥♥♥ ♥♥♥♥♥♥♥♥	
18	
	7

3.

♥♥♥♥♥♥♥♥♥ ♥♥♥♥♥	
8	7

4.

♥♥♥♥♥♥♥♥♥♥♥ ♥♥♥♥♥	
16	
	8

5.

♥♥♥♥♥♥♥♥♥♥ ♥♥♥♥	
14	
7	

6.

♥♥♥♥♥♥♥♥♥♥♥ ♥♥♥♥	
15	
6	

7.

♥♥♥♥♥♥♥♥♥♥♥ ♥♥♥♥♥♥	
9	8

8.

♥♥♥♥♥♥♥♥♥♥♥ ♥♥♥♥♥♥♥♥	
19	
14	

9.

♥♥♥♥♥♥♥♥♥ ♥♥♥♥♥♥	
16	
	7

WHAT'S MISSING?

Fill in the missing number in each table.

1.

17	
8	

2.

14	
	5

3.

6	8

4.

12	
	7

5.

5	8

6.

6	7

7.

19	
10	

8.

15	
	12

9.

16	
6	

MATH IN THE LIBRARY

Read the problems. Draw a picture to solve the problem.

1. The librarian put 16 books on one shelf and 3 books on another shelf. How many books did the librarian put on the shelves?

   _____

2. The librarian put 18 books on display. Villagers borrowed 9 books. How many books were left?

   _____

3. The librarian ordered 14 new books and 5 new maps. How many items did the librarian order?

   _____

4. There were 15 books on a shelf. The librarian put 7 of the books into a chest. How many books were left on the shelf?

   _____

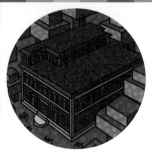

MATH IN THE WOODLAND MANSION

Read the problems. Draw a picture to solve the problem.

1. The villagers used redstone to build a jail. They used 17 blocks for one wall. They added 3 more blocks. How many blocks did they use?

   _____

2. The mansion has 15 windows on the first floor. 7 windows are broken. How many windows are not broken?

   _____

3. A player had 18 emeralds. She paid 12 emeralds for a map of the woodlands. How many emeralds did she have left?

   _____

4. The house has 13 flower pots. The player adds 6 more flower pots. How many flower pots are there?

   _____

FINDING TENS

Circle two numbers in the problem that equal 10.
Then add on the third number to solve.

1. $3 + 7 + 2 =$ _____

2. $2 + 6 + 8 =$ _____

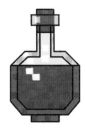

3. $4 + 1 + 6 =$ _____

4. $7 + 0 + 3 =$ _____

5. $3 + 5 + 5 =$ _____

6. $1 + 8 + 9 =$ _____

7. $8 + 2 + 4 =$ _____

8. $6 + 4 + 9 =$ _____

9. $5 + 6 + 5 =$ _____

10. $2 + 8 + 8 =$ _____

MYSTERY NUMBER CHALLENGE

Solve the problems. Identify the missing pair of numbers based on the clue.

1. The sum of the digits is 18, but their difference is 0.

_____ + _____ = 18   _____ - _____ = 0

2. The sum of the digits is 17, but the difference is 1.

_____ + _____ = 17   _____ - _____ = 1

3. The sum of the digits is 16, but the difference is 2.

_____ + _____ = 16   _____ - _____ = 2

4. The sum of the digits is 19, but the difference is 3.

_____ + _____ = 19   _____ - _____ = 3

NUMBERS TO 100

Fill in the missing numbers.

1									10
								19	
							28		
						37			
					46				
				55					
			64						
		73							
	82								
91									100

Patterns blow my mind!

PATTERNS TO 100

Follow the directions. Look for patterns.

1. Color the even numbers **yellow**.
2. Color 3 **blue**, then count by threes and color the numbers blue as you go. (3, 6, 9, 12 . . .)
3. Color 5 **green**, then count by fives and color the numbers green as you go. (5, 10, 15, 20 . . .)

1	2	3	4	5	6	7	8	9	10
11	12	13	14	15	16	17	18	19	20
21	22	23	24	25	26	27	28	29	30
31	32	33	34	35	36	37	38	39	40
41	42	43	44	45	46	47	48	49	50
51	52	53	54	55	56	57	58	59	60
61	62	63	64	65	66	67	68	69	70
71	72	73	74	75	76	77	78	79	80
81	82	83	84	85	86	87	88	89	90
91	92	93	94	95	96	97	98	99	100

PLACE VALUE WITHIN TENS

Count the tens and ones. Complete the chart.
The first one is done for you.

4 tens equals 40!

	Tens	Ones	Number
1.	4	8	48
2.			
3.			
4.			
5.			
6.			

EXPANDED NOTATION

Write each number in expanded form. The first one is done for you.

1. 38   30   +   8

2. 82   _____   +   _____

3. 44   _____   +   _____

4. 53   _____   +   _____

5. 67   _____   +   _____

6. 19   _____   +   _____

COMPARING NUMBERS

Use <, >, or = to compare the numbers.

< means less than
> means greater than
= means equal to

1. 15 $\boxed{<}$ 17   2. 33 $\boxed{\phantom{<}}$ 34

3. 72 $\boxed{\phantom{<}}$ 73   4. 43 $\boxed{\phantom{<}}$ 43

5. 32 $\boxed{\phantom{<}}$ 23   6. 91 $\boxed{\phantom{<}}$ 90

7. 41 $\boxed{\phantom{<}}$ 31   8. 59 $\boxed{\phantom{<}}$ 60

9. 62 $\boxed{\phantom{<}}$ 62   10. 28 $\boxed{\phantom{<}}$ 18

11. 60 $\boxed{\phantom{<}}$ 66   12. 85 $\boxed{\phantom{<}}$ 87

COMPARING EQUATIONS

Use <, >, or = to compare the numbers.

< means less than
> means greater than
= means equal to

1. 2 + 7 $\boxed{=}$ 3 + 6

2. 17 - 12 $\boxed{}$ 3 + 8

3. 10 + 5 $\boxed{}$ 7 + 7

4. 9 - 6 $\boxed{}$ 15 - 9

5. 12 - 7 $\boxed{}$ 13 - 8

6. 8 + 7 $\boxed{}$ 18 - 9

7. 9 + 9 $\boxed{}$ 18 - 9

8. 6 + 8 $\boxed{}$ 7 + 4

9. 17 - 8 $\boxed{}$ 11 - 2

10. 15 - 7 $\boxed{}$ 12 - 4

11. 8 + 5 $\boxed{}$ 12 + 7

12. 16 + 3 $\boxed{}$ 9 + 8

ADD WITHIN 100

Draw the numbers using lines for tens and dots for ones. Count the lines and dots to add. The first one is done for you.

		Tens	Ones
1.	43 + 24 ——— 67	|||| ||	● ● ● ● ● ● ●
2.	76 + 12 ———		
3.	51 + 20 ———		
4.	17 + 32 ———		
5.	62 + 26 ———		

ADD WITHIN 100

Solve the problems. Use the answers to help solve the riddle.

Q: Why are there no cars in Minecraft?

1.   24
     + 13
 	
 _____
 	
            H
	2. 56
	     + 32
	
	 _____
	
	            B
		3. 76
		     + 20
		
		 _____
		
		            T
			4. 12
			     + 36
			
			 _____
			
			            C

5.   33
     + 25
 	
 _____
 	
            E
	6. 31
	     + 12
	
	 _____
	
	            K
		7. 80
		     + 13
		
		 _____
		
		            O
			8. 62
			     + 23
			
			 _____
			
			            S

9.   14
     + 41
 	
 _____
 	
            D
	10. 12
	      + 22
	
	 _____
	
	            R
		11. 48
		      + 30
		
		 _____
		
		            A
			12. 31
			      + 42
			
			 _____
			
			            L

A:

_____ _____ _____
  96   37   58

_____ _____ _____ _____ _____ _____ _____
  85   96   34   58   58   96   85

_____ _____ _____
  78   34   58

_____ _____ _____ _____ _____ _____ _____
  88   73   93   48   43   58   55

SUBTRACT WITHIN 100

Draw lines and dots to show the first
number. Then cross out the second
number. Count the amount that's left.
The first one is done for you.

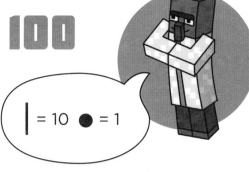

| = 10   ● = 1

1. 57
‑ 26
———
31

2. 78
‑ 37
———

3. 65
‑ 22
———

4. 84
‑ 41
———

5. 76
‑ 54
———

6. 49
‑ 15
———

SUBTRACT WITHIN 100

Solve the problems. Use the answers to help answer the riddle.

How did Steve describe making his first TNT tower? He said...

1. 78 − 44 S	2. 63 − 31 L	3. 96 − 53 B
4. 57 − 26 A	5. 82 − 20 T	6. 67 − 26 W
7. 49 − 27 I	8. 97 − 64 E	9. 88 − 34 R

___ ___   ___ ___ ___   ___
22   62   41   31   34   31

___ ___ ___ ___   ___ ___ ___ ___ ___ !
54   33   31   32   43   32   31   34   62

MULTIPLICATION

Solve the problems.

1. There are 4 Withers. Each Wither has 3 heads. How many heads altogether?

3 + 3 + 3 + 3 = _____

4 x 3 = _____

2. There are 2 rows of creepers attacking. Each row has 4 creepers. How many creepers altogether?

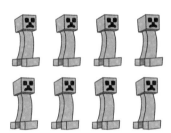

4 + 4 = _____

2 x 4 = _____

3. Ghasts have 9 legs. There are 3 ghasts. How many legs altogether?

9 + 9 + 9 = _____

9 x 3 = _____

4. There are 3 chickens. Each chicken laid 5 eggs. How many eggs altogether?

5 + 5 + 5 = _____

5 x 3 = _____

MINING MULTIPLICATION

Read the problem and look at the picture. Then solve it.

1. Steve found three piles of diamonds in the mine. Each pile had seven diamonds. How many diamonds did Steve find?

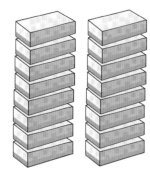

3 piles of 7 diamonds

3 x 7 = _____

2. Steve had four chests of emeralds. Each chest had five emeralds. How many emeralds did Steve have?

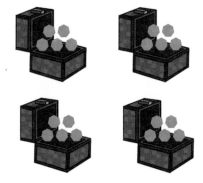

4 chests of 5 emeralds

4 x 5 = _____

3. Steve had two stacks of tin ingots. Each stack had eight tin ingots. How many tin ingots did Steve have?

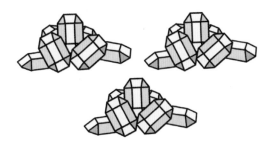

2 stacks of 8 tin ingots

2 x 8 = _____

4. Steve had three stacks of gold ingots. Each stack had five gold ingots. How many gold ingots did Steve have?

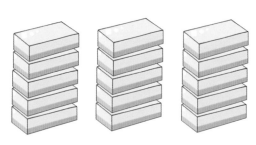

3 stacks of 5 gold ingots

3 x 5 = _____

MEASURING LENGTHS

Measure the lengths in inches.

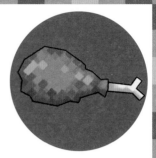

1. _____ inches

2. _____ inches

3. _____ inches

4. _____ inches

MEASURING LENGTHS

Measure the lengths in inches.

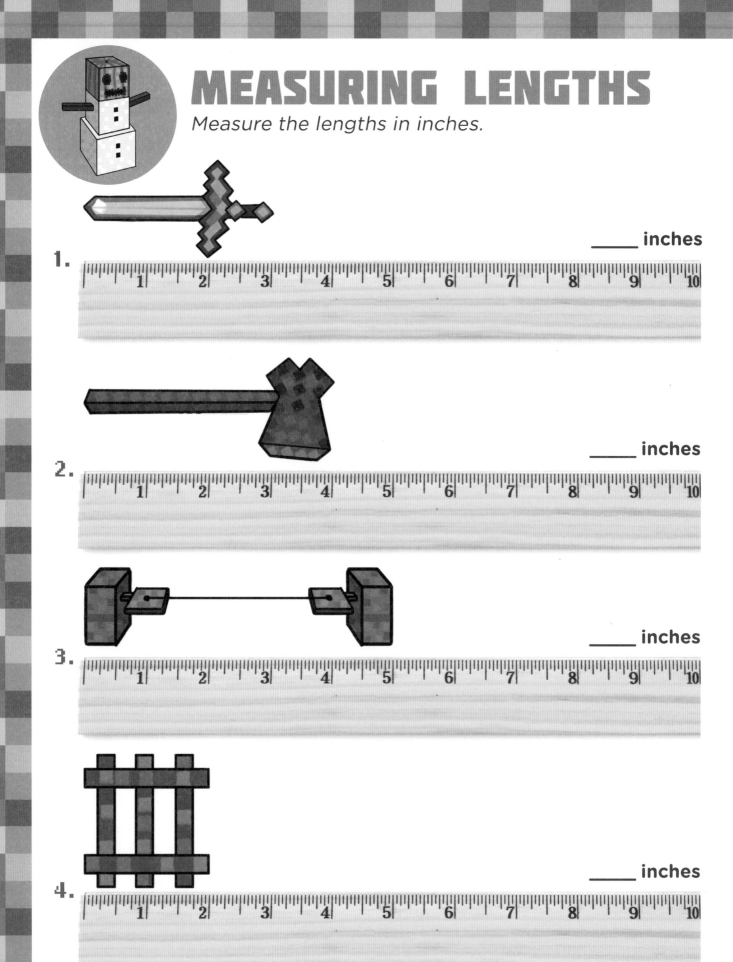

____ inches

1.

____ inches

2.

____ inches

3.

____ inches

4.

READING SCALES

Read the scale. Write the weight of the item(s) on the line.

1. _____ **ounces**

2. _____ **ounces**

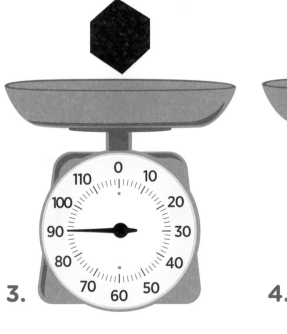

3. _____ **ounces**

4. _____ **ounces**

F stands for Fahrenheit. C stands for Celsius.

WHAT'S THE TEMPERATURE?

Read the thermometer. Write the temperature. Give your best guess.

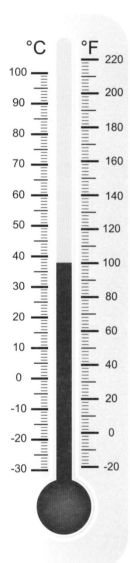

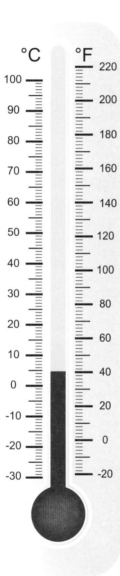

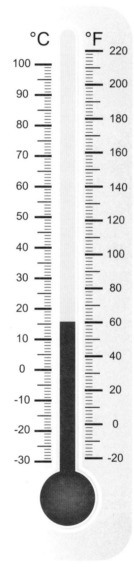

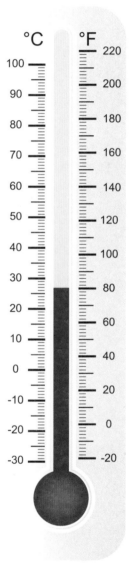

1.

_____ °F

_____ °C

2.

_____ °F

_____ °C

3.

_____ °F

_____ °C

4.

_____ °F

_____ °C

TELLING TIME

Look at the clocks. Write the time.

1.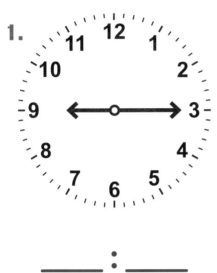

____ : ____

2.

____ : ____

3.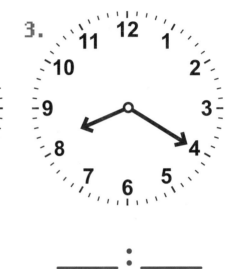

____ : ____

4.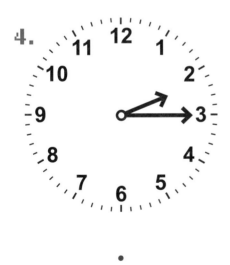

____ : ____

5.

____ : ____

6.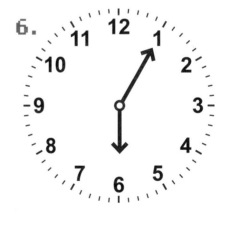

____ : ____

TELLING TIME

Look at the time. Draw the hands on the clock.

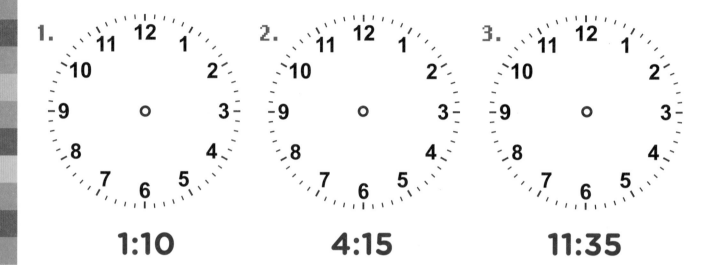

1. 1:10

2. 4:15

3. 11:35

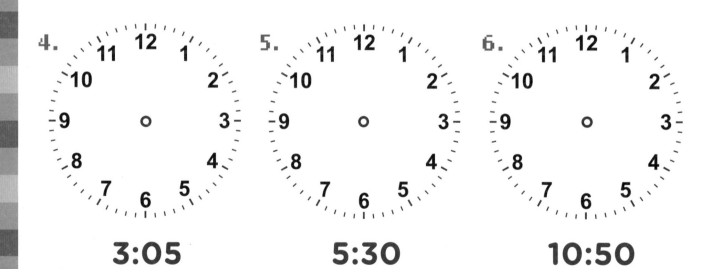

4. 3:05

5. 5:30

6. 10:50

COUNTING COINS

Add up the value of each group of coins.
Write the amount on the line.

1.  $\underline{\quad 50¢ \quad}$

2.  $\underline{\qquad}$

3.  $\underline{\qquad}$

4.  $\underline{\qquad}$

5.  $\underline{\qquad}$

6. $\underline{\qquad}$

MAKE A DOLLAR

Read the text box. Then show different ways to make a dollar. The first one is done for you.

Hint: Here are some ways to make a dollar.

4 quarters = $1.00	20 nickels = $1.00
10 dimes = $1.00	100 pennies = $1.00

1.

Q D D Q N Q

2.

3.

4.

5.

6.

MINECRAFTER'S CAFE

Look at the cost of each item at Minecrafter's cafe. Then match each snack to the correct amount of coins.

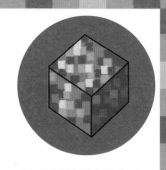

Minecrafter's Cafe

| 50¢ | 40¢ | 30¢ | 25¢ | 10¢ |

1.    A.

2.   B.

3.   C.

4.   D.

5.    E.

HOW MUCH CHANGE?

Each day Alex had $1.00 to spend on a snack. Look at what she bought and how much she paid. Then figure out her change.

Minecrafter's Cafe

 50¢   30¢   25¢   10¢

	Snacks Bought	Paid	Change
MONDAY		$1.00	
TUESDAY		$1.00	
WEDNESDAY		$1.00	
THURSDAY		$1.00	
FRIDAY		$1.00	

TWO-DIMENSIONAL SHAPES

Count the sides and corners of each shape. Record the information in the chart. Then draw each shape.

Shape	Sides	Corners	Draw the Shape
triangle			
rhombus			
rectangle			
circle			
square			
hexagon			
pentagon			
octagon			

Right angles connect two perpendicular straight lines.

FINDING SHAPES

Follow the directions to help the creeper learn about shapes.

1. **Color the shapes that have more than four sides** yellow**.**

2. **Color the shapes with four sides** green**.**

3. **Color the shapes with less than four sides** blue**.**

4. **Circle the squares.**

5. **Put a check mark next to the shapes that have right angles.**

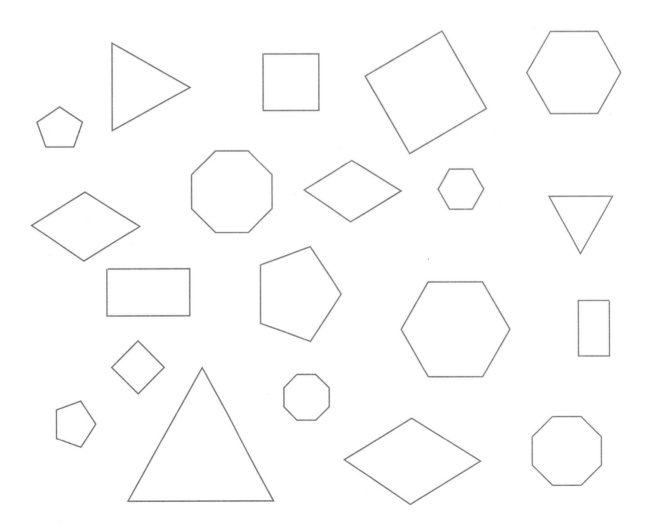

DRAWING SHAPES

Draw and name each shape.

hexagon   square   rectangle   triangle

1. Draw a shape that has three sides. Write its name.	**2.** Draw a shape that has four equal sides and four right angles. Write its name.
3. Draw a shape that has four right angles and four sides, including two pairs of equal sides. Write its name.	**4.** Draw a shape that has six sides. Write its name.

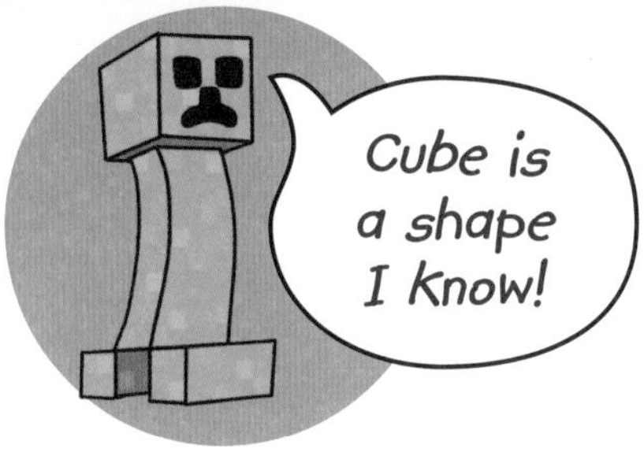
Cube is a shape I Know!

THREE-DIMENSIONAL SHAPES

Write the correct name for each shape. Write the number of faces each shape has.

triangular prism cube
cylinder rectangular prism

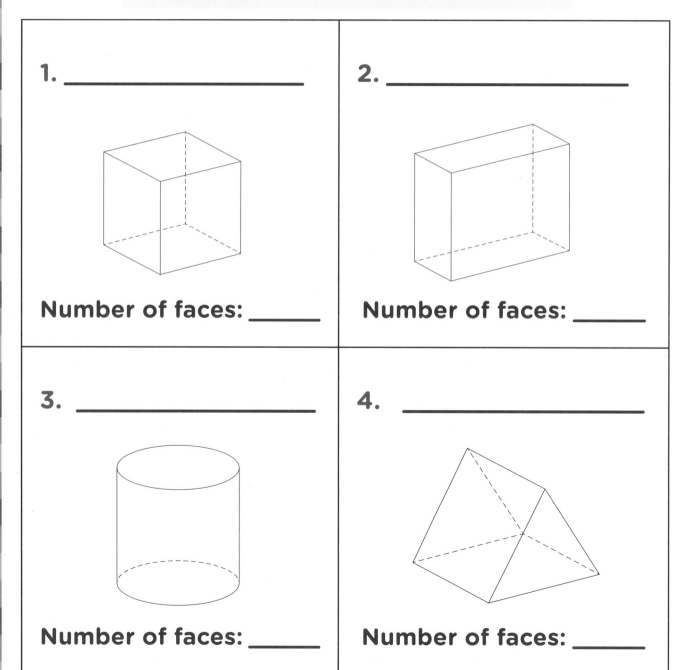

1. ____________________

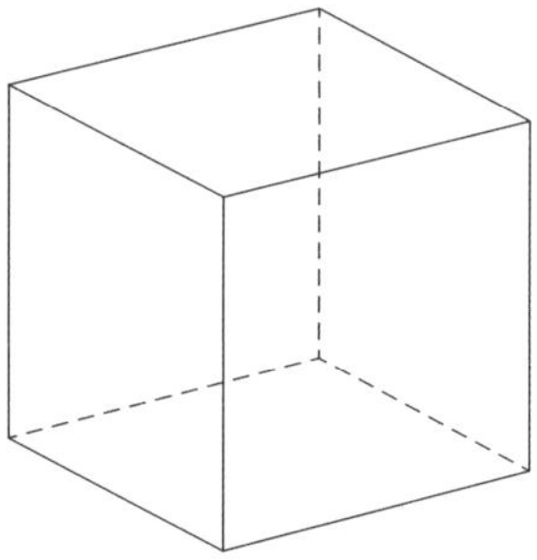

Number of faces: _____

2. ____________________

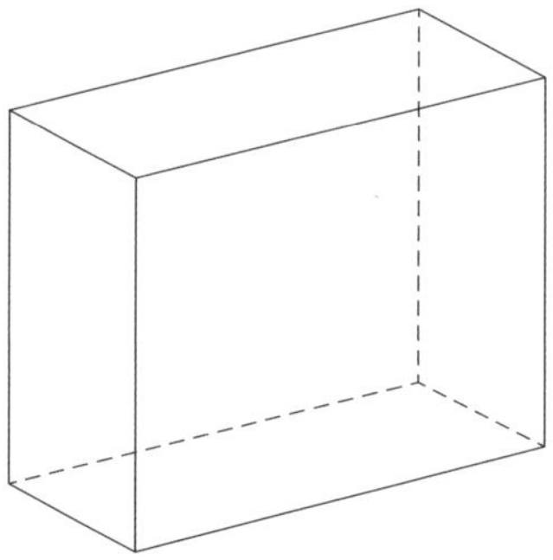

Number of faces: _____

3. ____________________

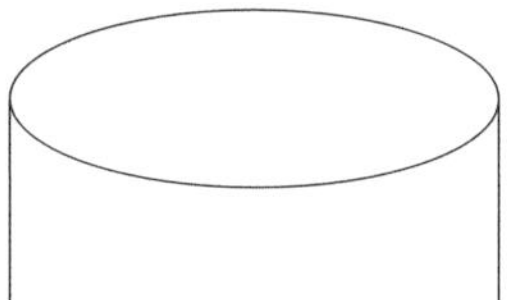

Number of faces: _____

4. ____________________

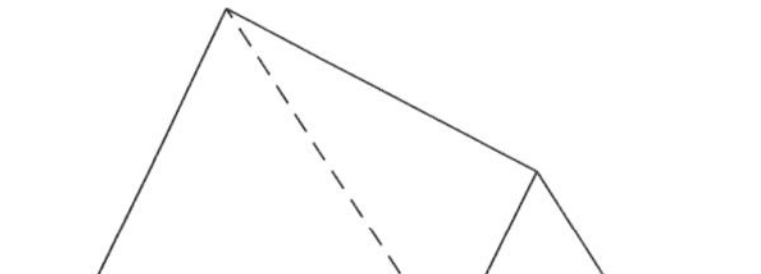

Number of faces: _____

EQUAL PARTS

Draw lines to partition the shapes.
Count the equal parts.

1.

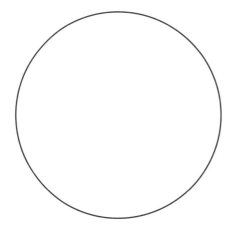

Two equal parts =

_____ halves

2.

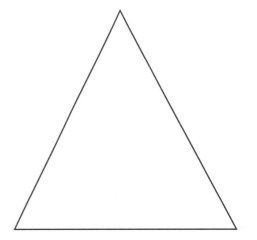

Two equal parts =

_____ halves

3.

Three equal parts =

_____ thirds

4.

Four equal parts =

_____ fourths

EQUAL PARTS-DIFFERENT WAYS

Draw lines to partition each shape in two different ways.

1. **two parts or halves**

2. **three parts or thirds**

3. **four parts or fourths**

4. **two parts or halves**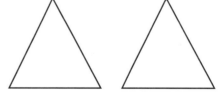

5. **two parts or halves**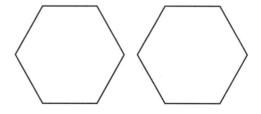

WHERE DID IT COME FROM?

*Write an **N** if the item is natural.*
*Write a **P** if the item is made by people.*

Everything that you see is either natural or made by people. Natural things are found in nature. People do not make natural things. For example, water is natural. People do not make water. People make many things to make life easier.

1. _____

2. _____

3. _____

4. _____

5. _____

6. _____

7. _____

8. _____

Materials are used to make new things.

WHAT'S IT MADE OF?

Write the material used to make each item.

MATERIALS

plastic   fabric   metal   glass   rubber   wood

1. _____

2. _____

3. _____

4. _____

5. _____

6. _____

7. _____

8. _____

9. _____

MATERIALS ALL AROUND

Look around the room. Draw something that is made with each type of material.

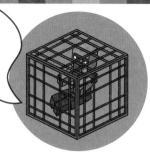

This monster spawner is made of iron.

made of fabric	**made of glass**
made of metal	**made of wood**
made of rubber	**made of plastic**

WHAT'S THE MATTER?

*Read about matter. Then write an **L** if the item is liquid, **S** if the item is solid, or **G** if the item is gas.*

Matter is anything that takes up space and has mass. Matter can be a liquid like water, a solid like ice, or a gas like steam. **Liquids** are wet. They do not have a shape. They take on the shape of their container. **Solids** are hard and have their own shape. Gases do not have a shape. **Gases** are mostly invisible.

1. ____ lava	2. ____ gold	3. ____ breath
4. ____ book	5. ____ water	6. ____ potion
7. ____ armor	8. ____ cookie	9. ____ bubbles

PROPERTIES OF MATTER

Read about matter. Circle the words that are a property of the item.

All matter has **properties**. A property is a way to describe an object. Some properties include color, shape, size, texture, and weight.

1. gold ingot	yellow hard round light	
2. stick	triangular brown soft square	
3. sugar	stretchy white sweet light	
4. web	heavy sticky rough stringy	
5. gems	soft green smooth sticky	

SOURCES OF LIGHT

Light is a source of energy. Circle the things that give light.

94

LET THE LIGHT SHINE IN

Cross out the material in each group that does NOT belong.

Light can pass through some materials. Materials can be transparent, translucent, or opaque. **Transparent** materials let ALL light pass through. **Translucent** materials let SOME light pass through. **Opaque** materials let NO light pass through.

Transparent	Translucent	Opaque

SUN

*Read about the sun. Write **T** by the sentences that are true. Write **F** by the sentences that are false.*

The sun is a star. It is larger than Earth, but smaller than other stars. It looks big because it is the closest star to Earth. The sun never stops shining. Earth turns on its axis and revolves around the sun. When Earth turns away from the sun, it is nighttime. When it is facing the sun, it is daytime. It takes Earth one day to turn on its axis. The sun gives heat and light to the Earth. Without the sun, there would be no life on Earth. Sunlight gives plants energy to grow.

_____ 1. The sun is a star.

_____ 2. The sun revolves around Earth.

_____ 3. At night, the sun stops shining.

_____ 4. The sun gives us heat and light.

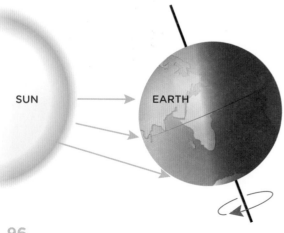

SUN   EARTH

STARS

Do stars look like small lights in the sky? Stars are large balls of fiery gas. The North Star is a very bright star. Long ago, people used the North Star and groups of stars called **constellations** to find their way home. Connect the dots to show some star constellations.

1. Big Dipper

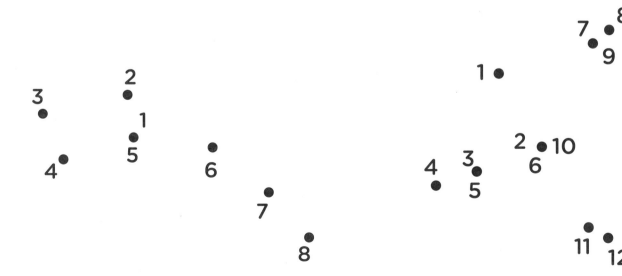

2. Little Dipper

3. Aquila (eagle)

OUR MOON

*Read about the moon. Then color the parts of the moon marked **B** in black and the parts marked **Y** in yellow to show the phases of the moon.*

Our Moon

The moon is a satellite. It moves around the Earth. It is smaller than the Earth. The moon is a big ball of rock. It is dry and rocky. The moon gets its light from the sun. It does not have its own light. The sun can only shine on one area of the moon's surface at a time. That is why the moon looks like it changes shape. The changes in the way the moon looks are called phases of the moon.

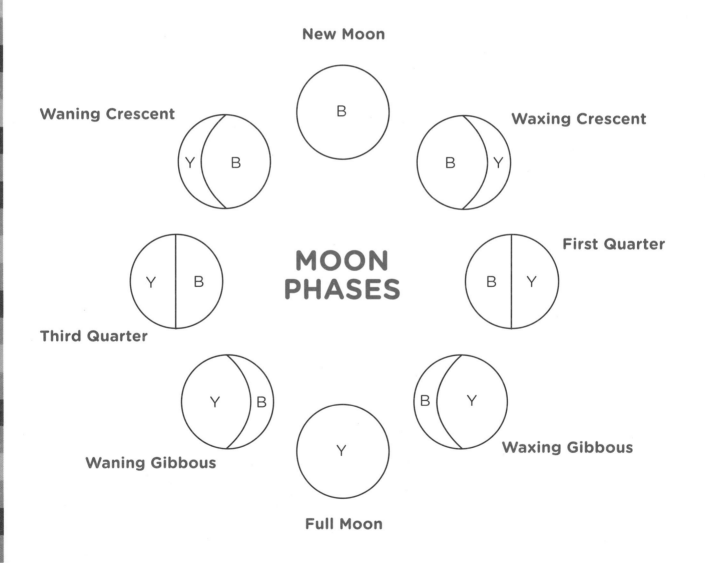

MAN ON THE MOON

I would like to walk on the moon.

Read about the first moon landing. Then circle the words in the puzzle.

About 50 years ago, *Apollo 11* landed on the moon. This spacecraft carried three astronauts: Neil Armstrong, Buzz Aldrin, and Michael Collins. Armstrong and Aldrin walked on the moon. They had to wear space suits. The suits gave them oxygen. They collected moon dust. They left a U.S. flag.

Neil Armstrong	astronaut	U.S. flag
Buzz Aldrin	space suit	dust
Michael Collins	spacecraft	*Apollo 11*
moon		

B N E I L A R M S T R O N G Z U

U Z A L O N T O L S P U O 1 1 S

Z U A P O L L O 1 1 A E P S P F

Z E L I L U I N R I C O R S U L

A B A S T R O N A U T H R P B A

L C R S P A C E S U I T L A U G

D U S T D E O O I A T 1 1 I S T

R E M I C H A E L C O L L I N S

I C S P A C E C R A F T M C L E

N H B U D W T O W A C O N H O S

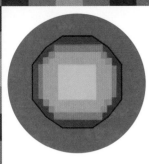

OUR SOLAR SYSTEM

Look at this drawing of our solar system. Use the clues on the next page to label the sun and the planets.

Use the clues to label the sun and the planets on page 100.

Hint: Use the white rings to figure out how far each planet is from the sun.

1. **The sun is in the center of our solar system. All the planets revolve around the sun.**

2. **Mercury is the planet closest to the sun.**

3. **Neptune is the planet farthest from the sun.**

4. **Earth is the only planet known to have life. It has water and land. It is the third planet from the sun.**

5. **Mars is known for its red color.**

6. **Venus is the second planet from the sun.**

7. **Saturn and Uranus are known for their rings. Saturn is closer to the sun than Uranus.**

8. **Jupiter is the largest planet.**

PLANET EARTH

Circle the words that make Earth the perfect place for humans and animals to live.

continents	Earth
oceans	sun
mountains	tides
sky	moon
islands	plants
deserts	trees
jungles	water

```
T E M O U N T A I N S E
J P L A N T S N R W U L
U A U M O O N O W A N I
N S R O C E A N S T U S
G E T I D E S L K E R L
L R L G I O V J Y R C A
E A R T H E T R E E S N
S E F R O W I U N S D D
O C O N T I N E N T S S
R T D E S E R T S E I N
```

CREATE A PLANET FOR MINECRAFTERS

Create a Minecrafting-themed planet. Draw some Minecraft landforms on the planet. Answer the questions to describe the planet.

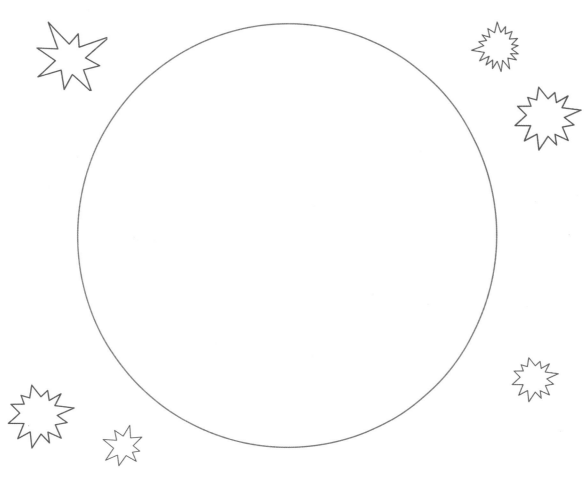

Planet's name: _____

Planet's location in space: _____

What it's like to live there: _____

_____

WATER

Water is essential for life on Earth. Read about how water changes. Look at the diagram. Then, answer the questions.

Water changes. Ice is solid water. When ice warms up, it changes to liquid water. The water you drink is liquid. When liquid water warms up, it turns to water vapor. Water vapor is a gas.

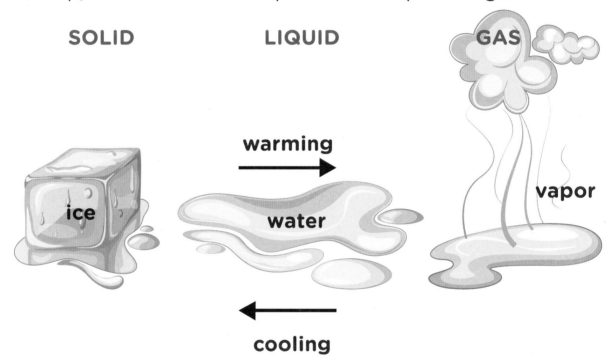

SOLID   **LIQUID**   **GAS**

warming

ice   water   vapor

cooling

1. Solid water is called _____

2. When ice melts, it becomes _____

3. When water heats up, it becomes _____

4. When water vapor cools, it becomes _____

5. When water freezes, it becomes _____

THE WATER CYCLE

Read about the water cycle. Look at the diagram. Answer the questions.

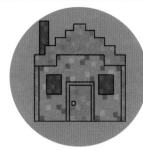

Water is always moving. When the sun heats the water in the ocean, it turns to water vapor. This is called **evaporation**. The vapor rises and creates condensation. **Condensation** makes clouds. When the clouds are heavy with water, they become precipitation. **Precipitation** is rain, hail, sleet, or snow. The precipitation falls to the ground. It returns to the ocean. This is the water cycle.

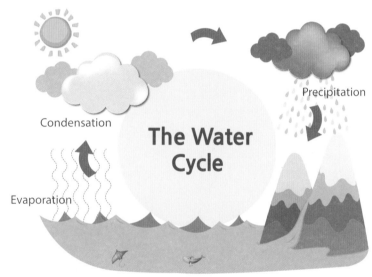

1. What happens when water heats and rises?

_____

2. What makes the clouds?

_____

3. What is another word for rain and snow?

_____

HOW PLANTS GET FOOD

Read about how plants get food. Then label the diagram with the three things that help plants make their own food.

Every living thing needs food to grow. Plants make their own food. They use energy from the sun, carbon dioxide from the air, and water to make food. This process is called photosynthesis. During photosynthesis, plants produce sugars that they use for food. They also produce oxygen that humans need to breathe.

carbon dioxide   energy   water

1. _____

2. _____

3. _____

SEEDS AND PLANTS

Minecrafters know that lots of important things start out as seeds. Draw a line to match the seeds below to the correct plant.

1.

An apple seed grows into an apple tree.

A.

2.

A pine cone grows into a pine tree.

B.

3.

A corn kernel grows into a stalk.

C.

4.

An acorn grows into an oak tree.

D.

HOW SEEDS TRAVEL

*Read about how seeds travel. Then write **T** if the sentence is true and **F** if it is false.*

Seeds come from plants, and plants come from seeds. Each plant has its own special seed. People plant seeds. Seeds move in different ways. The wind moves some seeds. Water and animals also move seeds. Some seeds stick to animals' fur. Other seeds are eaten by animals. Some animals bury seeds in the ground. Eventually, the seed will grow into a plant.

_____ Seeds come from plants.

_____ People plant seeds.

_____ The sun moves seeds.

_____ Seeds stick to animals' fur.

_____ Seeds always stay in one place.

LIFE CYCLE OF AN APPLE TREE

Look at the diagram. Use the words in the word box to complete the sentences and describe the life cycle of an apple tree.

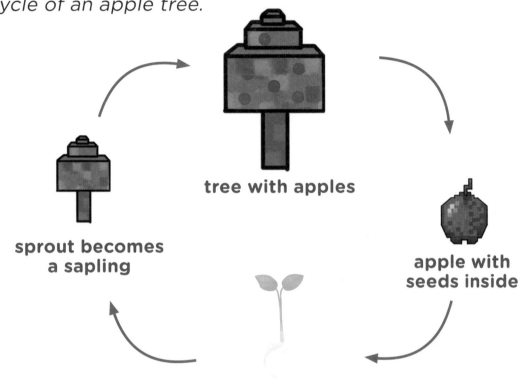

tree with apples

sprout becomes
a sapling

apple with
seeds inside

seed becomes a sprout

tree	apples	sapling	seeds	sprout

First, an apple tree grows _____. Inside

an apple are _____. A seed becomes a _____.

The sprout becomes a _____. The sapling grows

into a _____.

INSECTS

Read about insects. Not all of the creatures below are insects. Circle the ones that are insects.

Insects are a small animals. There are many different types of insects. Insects have three body parts: the head, thorax, and abdomen. The head often has eyes, a mouth, and antennae. The antennae help the insect sense where it is going. The thorax has legs and sometimes wings. Insects have six legs. All insects have six legs, but not all insects have wings.

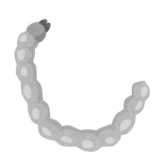

HOUSEFLIES

Read about the housefly. Then label its parts.

The housefly is an insect. It has six legs. It also has three body parts: the head, the thorax, and the abdomen. The head has the eyes and antennae. The thorax is the middle part. It has the legs and the wings. The third part is the abdomen.

abdomen   antennae   eye
head   leg   thorax   wings

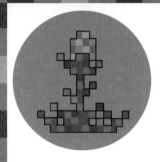

LIFE CYCLE OF A BUTTERFLY

Read about the butterfly. Then use the words in the word box to label the life cycle of a butterfly.

The life cycle of a butterfly has four stages: egg, larva, pupa, and adult. Butterfly eggs are very small. Inside the egg, the caterpillar or larva grows. When it hatches, the caterpillar begins to eat. It eats a lot. When it is big enough, it will form into a chrysalis or pupa. Inside the pupa, the caterpillar changes into an adult butterfly.

adult	egg	larva	pupa

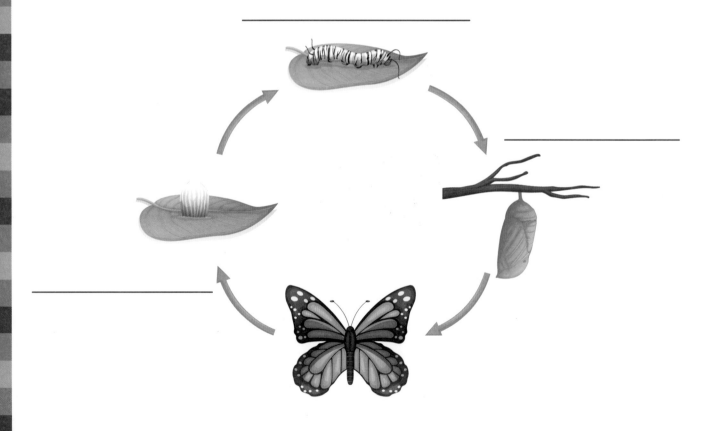

SPIDERS

Read about spiders. Draw a spider in the box below and label the parts you know.

Spiders are not insects. They are arachnids. They have eight legs. They have two body parts – the cephalothorax and the abdomen. The **cephalothorax** is the front part of a spider. This part has its brains and eyes. Most spiders have eight eyes. The **abdomen** is behind the cephalothorax. It holds the spider's lungs.

LIFE CYCLE OF A CHICKEN

Look at the diagram of the life cycle of a chicken.
Write the correct numbers on the lines.

1. The chick hatches.

2. The chick becomes a chicken.

3. The chicken lays an egg.

4. The embryo grows inside the egg.

5. The chick grows.

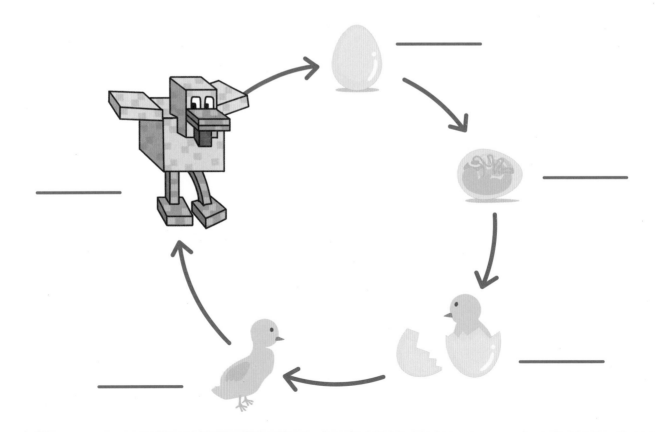

FOOD CHAINS

Look at the food chains below. The arrows show who eats what. Draw an animal to complete each food chain.

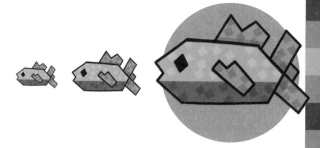

Everything needs energy to live. Plants get energy from the sun. Animals and people get energy from plants and other animals. This is called the food chain. A food chain shows how living things depend on other living things for food.

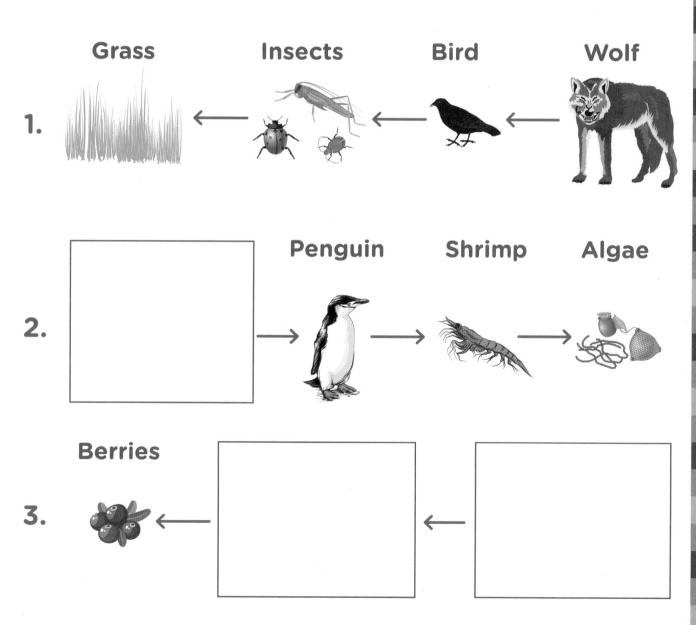

Grass   **Insects**   **Bird**   **Wolf**

1.

Penguin   **Shrimp**   **Algae**

2.

Berries

3.

I use my speed to survive.

HOW ANIMALS SURVIVE

Animals have many different ways to protect themselves. They can use their bodies to hide, fight back, or shield themselves. Draw a line from each animal to the way it protects itself.

1.

2.

3.

4.

5.

A. hard shell

B. sharp teeth and claws

C. special coloring

D. bad smell

E. blend in with their environment

HOW ANIMALS SURVIVE WINTER

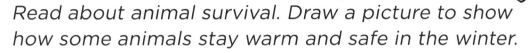

Read about animal survival. Draw a picture to show how some animals stay warm and safe in the winter.

Animals have different ways of surviving cold winters. Reindeer, birds, and butterflies **migrate**. They move to warmer places. Bears and some bees **hibernate**, or sleep, through winter in a cave or hollowed-out tree. Other animals, like squirrels and rabbits, **adapt** to survive. They eat more to develop an extra layer of fat or they grow thicker fur.

SIMPLE MACHINES

Minecrafters build machines to help them do work. See if you can find the simple machines in the picture below. Then read about simple machines to learn more.

Do you see the shovel in this picture? It is a **lever** that helps us lift things. There is an axe in this picture as well. It splits wood apart, so it is called a **wedge**. *Circle those images above.* **Inclined planes** are ramps that allow us to roll heavy things up and down. A **screw** holds things together as it spirals up or down.

SIMPLE MACHINES

Look at the examples of simple machines. Help Steve match each simple machine to its name.

1.

      a. wedge

2.

      b. lever

3.

      c. screw

4.

      d. inclined plane

MY CULTURE

Culture is the way a group of people live. Draw or write information about the culture of your family.

Where we live

How we dress

What we eat

Our language

Our celebrations

ANOTHER CULTURE

Research the culture of another country. Draw or write information about that country's culture.

Country where they live

How they dress

What they eat

Their language

Their celebrations

SHOWING RESPECT

When you treat your teachers, family, and classmates with respect, you get respect in return. Check each example of showing respect to someone.

☐ 1. obeying the rules

☐ 2. listening when someone is talking

☐ 3. laughing at someone

☐ 4. cleaning up after yourself

☐ 5. talking over someone

☐ 6. cutting someone in line

☐ 7. playing only with kids like you

☐ 8. refusing to do homework

☐ 9. looking for the good in others

☐ 10. saying you're sorry if you hurt someone's feelings

☐ 11. insisting on doing things your way

HEALTHY MIND AND BODY

Healthy habits help you feel good all day long. Your mind and your body need exercise, sleep, good foods, and fun activities. Draw and write about one of your healthy habits below.

exercise

find time to relax

eat good foods

have a hobby

I feel my best when I _____

_____

BE A GOOD FRIEND

Read the statements. Check true if it is something a good friend would do. Check false if it is not something a good friend would do.

1. A good friend says "hi" when they see you.

   True ☐ False ☐

2. A good friend knows your name.

   True ☐ False ☐

3. A good friend listens to you.

   True ☐ False ☐

4. A good friend doesn't want to do anything you want to do.

   True ☐ False ☐

5. A good friend gives you high fives.

   True ☐ False ☐

6. A good friend pushes you.

   True ☐ False ☐

7. A good friend gets mad when you don't do things his or her way.

   True ☐ False ☐

8. A good friend smiles at you.

   True ☐ False ☐

MY FRIENDSHIP CHART

To have a good friend, you need to be a good friend. Complete the chart with ways you can be a good friend.

A good friend

is	can	will

I will be a friend to _____.

I love to celebrate birthdays!

FAMILY CELEBRATIONS

Families have celebrations to remember dates that are important to them. Draw a picture and write about a family celebration that you enjoyed.

My favorite family celebration is _____

My family celebrates by _____

_____

U.S. HOLIDAYS

In the United States, we have holidays to remember important people or events in our history. Match each picture to the name of the holiday.

1.

to remember those who fought for our country

2.

to honor our presidents

3.

to honor workers

4.

to celebrate our independence

A. Independence Day
July 4th

B. Memorial Day
Last Monday in May

C. Labor Day
1st Monday in September

D. Presidents' Day
3rd Monday in February

PEOPLE TO KNOW: GEORGE WASHINGTON

Read about George Washington. Then circle the words in the puzzle that tell about his life.

George Washington was the first president of the United States. Before he was president, he led the Army. He helped the colonies gain freedom. When the colonies were free, they joined together to become the United States. Washington also helped to figure out the laws of our country. He worked hard to help our country. He is known as the Father of Our Country.

president	Father of	Martha Washington
army general	Our Country	leader
mapmaker	Virginia	six feet tall
	Mount Vernon	

```
M  A  L  R  O  P  D  W  A  S  R  K  E  R  A  L  L  T
F  A  T  H  E  R  O  F  O  U  R  C  O  U  N  T  R  Y
M  O  L  I  L  E  A  D  E  R  I  N  G  R  M  A  K  M
O  A  A  R  M  S  I  X  F  E  E  T  T  A  L  L  N  A
S  I  R  M  V  I  R  G  I  N  I  A  T  O  N  E  E  P
P  C  O  U  R  D  M  Y  F  A  T  I  S  E  P  R  E  M
A  R  M  Y  G  E  N  E  R  A  L  E  E  R  A  L  K  A
P  E  M  O  U  N  T  V  E  R  N  O  N  A  G  R  T  K
A  E  R  C  O  T  U  F  A  E  E  R  I  N  S  H  G  E
M  M  A  R  T  H  A  W  A  S  H  I  N  G  T  O  N  R
```

PEOPLE TO KNOW: ABRAHAM LINCOLN

Read about Abraham Lincoln. Then unscramble the words to complete the sentences.

Abraham Lincoln was the 16th president. He was a strong leader. When he was president, our country disagreed on many things. Many states in the south did not want to be part of the United States. The states in the north and the states in the south went to war. This war is known as the Civil War. During the war, Lincoln signed a law to end slavery.

1. Lincoln was the 16th _____.

ESRNPIEDT

2. Lincoln was the president during

the _____ War.

LICIV

3. Lincoln signed a law to end _____.

RYLEVAS

4. Lincoln was a strong _____.

DELARE

She's brave like me!

PEOPLE TO KNOW: SUSAN B. ANTHONY

Read about Susan B. Anthony. Then answer the question.

Women have not always had the right to vote. Women were not allowed to vote for either George Washington or Abraham Lincoln. But Susan B. Anthony worked hard to get women the right to vote. She gave many speeches and wrote many newspaper articles. Many other women worked hard, too. Today women can vote. A dollar coin was made to honor Susan B. Anthony.

What did Susan B. Anthony do to help women?

_____

_____

_____

_____

PEOPLE TO KNOW: MARTIN LUTHER KING JR.

History is my favorite subject!

Read about Martin Luther King, Jr. Then finish the sentence with something you hope for our country.

Martin Luther King, Jr. fought for equal rights. He fought for the rights of African Americans. He lived in a time when laws didn't allow African Americans the same rights as white Americans. He made a famous speech known as the "I Have a Dream" speech. King had a dream that all people would be treated equally.

I have a dream that ... _____

_____

_____

_____

_____

_____

SCHOOL RULES

Rules are important in every part of life. Rules help people live together. Write about the rules you have at home and at school in each circle. Are there any rules that are the same? If so, write them in the center.

Rules at School

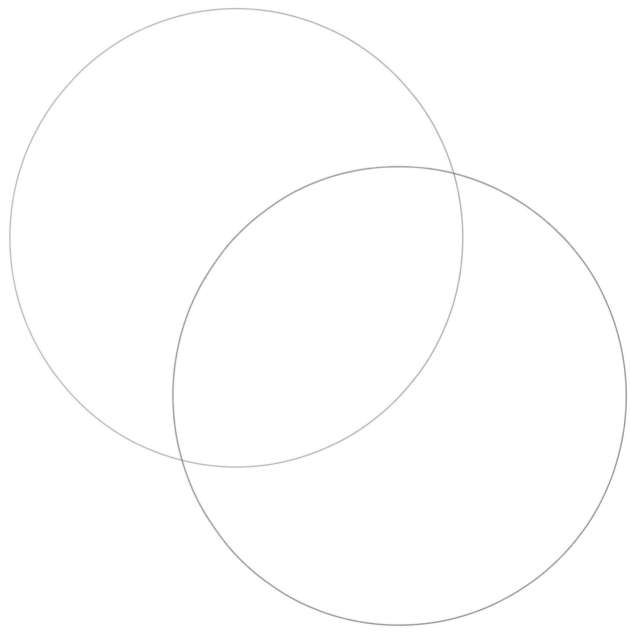

Rules at Home

WHO MAKES THE RULES?

I will fight for the rules. Rules help keep us safe.

Think about the rules you have. Complete the chart.

	Family	School
Who Makes the Rules?		
What Happens If the Rules Are Broken?		
How Do the Rules Help?		

LAWS IN OUR COUNTRY

Read about laws in the United States. Then use the clues to complete the crossword on the next page.

Laws are like rules. They help people live in peace. Three branches or groups work together to make the laws fair. The legislative branch is made up of senators and representatives from every state. They make the laws. The executive branch makes sure that people follow the laws. The president is the head of the executive branch. The judicial branch includes the judges and the courts. They decide if a person has broken a law. The judge decides the punishment for people who break the law.

Across

1 a person who makes the laws

6 number of branches of government

8 citizens _____ vote

9 branch that decides the punishment for people who break the law

10 branch that makes the laws

12 a person who makes the laws

Down

2 head of the executive branch

3 All people are created _____.

4 branch that makes people follow the laws

5 group of government

7 a person on the judicial branch

11 rules

legislative
executive
judicial
branch

president
senator
representative
laws

judge
three

U.S. MONUMENTS

Minecrafters battle guardians to explore ocean monuments. The United States has monuments and important buildings, too. Match each monument or building with its name.

1. Statue of Liberty

A.

2. Mount Rushmore

B.

3. Washington Monument

C.

4. U.S. Capitol Building

D.

5. Lincoln Memorial

E.

MY STATE

Look up information in a book or on the Internet about your state. Draw pictures to tell about your state.

I live in _____.

write the name of your state

My State	**State Flag**
State Bird	**State Flower**

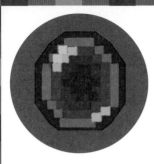

MAP OF THE UNITED STATES
Read the map. Answer the questions.

1. How many states does the United States have?

_____

2. What two states are not connected to the other states?

_____   _____

3. Name a state that borders the Pacific Ocean.

_____

4. Name a state that borders the Atlantic Ocean.

_____

5. Name a state that borders Canada.

_____

6. Name a state that borders Mexico.

_____

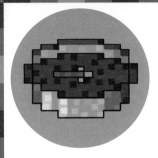

READING A MAP COMPASS

Read about compasses. Then fill in the blanks to complete the sentences.

A compass is used to help people find places. A compass rose like the one below is used on a map to show direction. The letters on the compass tell you which way is north, south, east, and west.

north   south   east   west

1. On a map, the tower flame is pointing _____.

2. The Ender Dragon is flying _____.

3. The Enderman is walking _____.

4. Steve is heading _____ in his mine cart.

NORTH AMERICA

The United States is on the continent of North America. Read the map. Answer the questions.

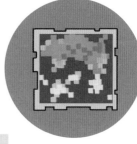

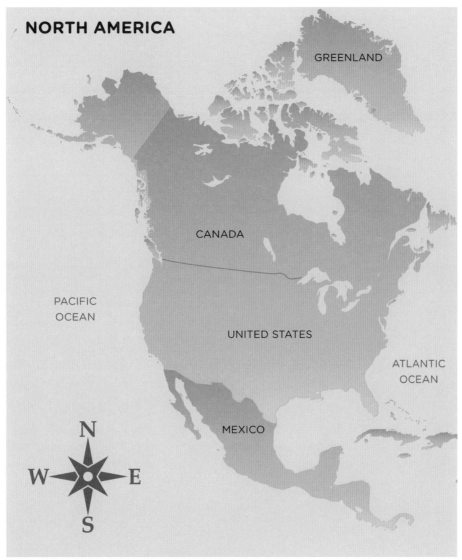

NORTH AMERICA

GREENLAND

CANADA

PACIFIC OCEAN

UNITED STATES

ATLANTIC OCEAN

MEXICO

N W E S

1. **Draw a flag on the United States.**

2. **Place an X where you live.**

3. **What country is north of the U.S.?**

_____

4. **What ocean is on the east coast of the U.S.?**

_____

FAMOUS PLACES AROUND THE WORLD

Read about some famous places in countries around the world. Then find the country and write the number on the map on page 143. The first one is done for you.

1.

The Statue of Liberty is in the United States. It is a symbol of freedom.

2.

The Sphinx is in Egypt. It was built over 4,500 years ago. It is 241 feet high.

3.

The Leaning Tower of Pisa is in Italy. It is a bell tower. It leans because of the soft soil it was built on.

4.

The Great Wall of China is the longest wall in the world. It is over 13,000 miles long.

5.

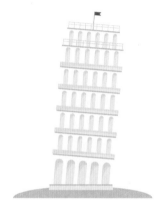

The Taj Mahal is in India. It was built by the emperor to honor his wife.

6.

Machu Picchu is in Peru. It is an ancient city that was undiscovered for hundreds of years.

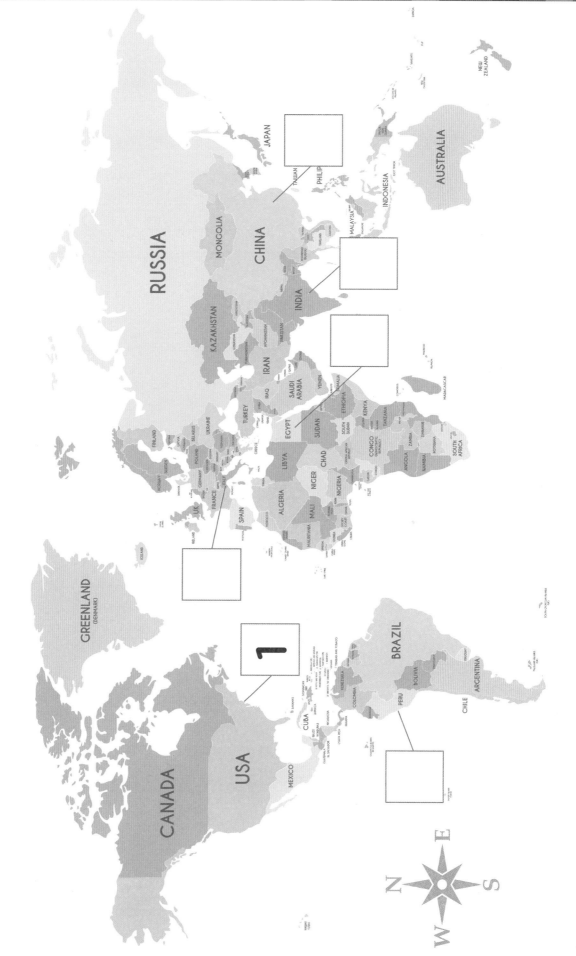

OUR WORLD

The mobs are taking over the world. Look at the map. Name each continent.

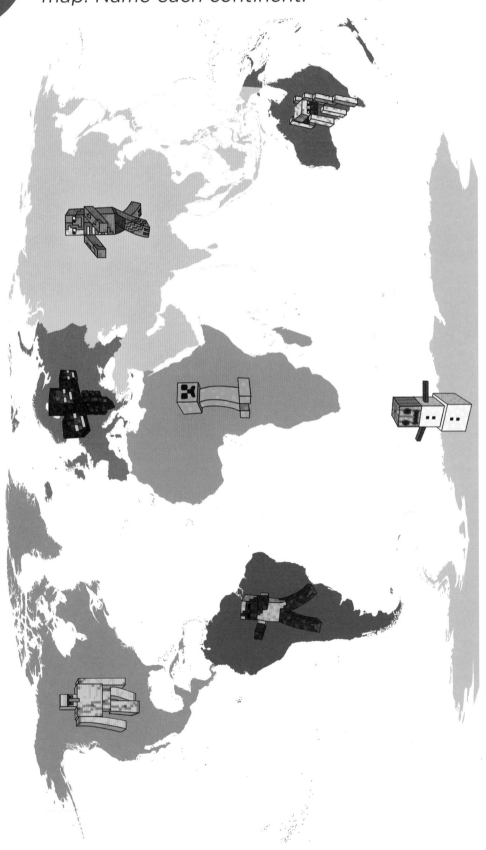

Africa   Antarctica   Asia   Australia   Europe
North America   South America

1. Where is ? _____

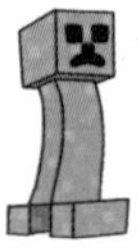

2. Where is ? _____

3. Where is ? _____

4. Where is ? _____

5. Where is ? _____

6. Where is ? _____

7. Where is ? _____

ON THE FARM

Read the map of the farm. Then follow the directions.

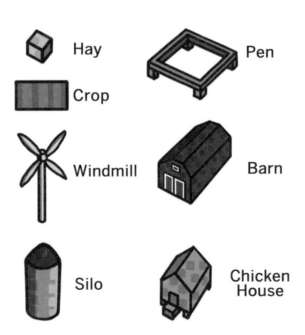

Hay

Crop

Windmill

Silo

Pen

Barn

Chicken
House

1. **Draw an X on the hay bales.**

2. **Draw a circle around the silos.**

3. **Draw a triangle around the windmills.**

4. **Draw a line from the barn to a chicken house.**

5. **Draw three animals you might find on a farm.**

Whoever invented computers was a genius!

THEN AND NOW

Things are always changing. People invent new ways to make life easier. Look at some of the things from long ago. Draw a line from each item to what we used today.

Then

1.

2.

3.

4.

5.

Now

A.

B.

C.

D.

E.

MAKE A TIMELINE

Creeper made a timeline of his life. Can you make a timeline of all the important moments in your life? Start with the year you were born and the year you started school. Add other important dates like when you learned to walk, when you lost your first tooth, and other exciting moments you remember.

Creeper's Life

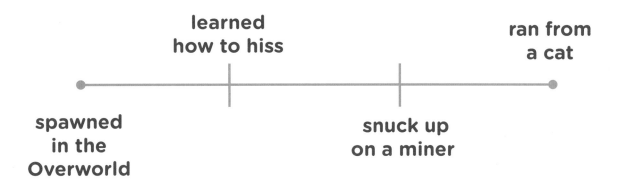

learned
how to hiss

ran from
a cat

spawned
in the
Overworld

snuck up
on a miner

My Life

ANSWER KEY

PAGE 5

1. short; 2. long; 3. short; 4. short; 5. long;
6. long; 7. short; 8. short; 9. long

PAGE 6

1. long; 2. short; 3. long; 4. long; 5. short;
6. short; 7. short; 8. long; 9. short

PAGE 7

1. C; 2. D; 3. E; 4. B; 5. A

PAGE 8

Answers will vary.

PAGE 9

1. th; 2. sh; 3. ch; 4. ch; 5. sh; 6. sh; 7. th;
8. ch; 9. th

PAGE 10

1. D; 2. A; 3. F; 4. B; 5. C; 6. E

PAGE 11

1. slime; 2. cake; 3. rose; 4. cube; 5. blaze

PAGE 12

1. goat; 2. tail; 3. pie; 4. beet; 5. meat; 6. blue

PAGE 13

1. snow golem; 2. night; 3. play; 4. fight;
5. glowstone; 6. hay; 7. daylight sensor;
8. day; 9. rowboat

PAGE 14

PAGE 15

1. replay, D; 2. unopened, C; 3. premix, A;
4. retry, E; 5. unhappy, B

PAGE 16

1. fearless, D; 2. villager, C; 3. joyful, B;
4. creeper, E; 5. fearful, A

PAGE 17

1. pork / chop; 2. puffer / fish; 3. red / stone;
4. beet / root; 5. chest / plate; 6. swamp /
land; 7. pick / axe; 8. glow / stone; 9. fire /
ball

PAGE 18

1. pigman; 2. drumstick; 3. doorknob;
4. silverfish; 5. Enderman

PAGE 19

1. 1; 2. 2; 3. 1; 4. 1; 5. 1; 6. 3; 7. 3; 8. 4

PAGE 20

1. mush / room; 2. com / pass; 3. cac / tus;
4. rab / bit; 5. sad / dle; 6. ban / ner;
7. with / er; 8. an / vil

PAGE 21

1. one who takes care of; 2. blocks;
3. made; 4. hides away

PAGE 22

1. a world above the ground; 2. arms and legs; 3. bothered; 4. not able to be seen; 5. to move away

PAGE 23

1. The creeper explodes. D; 2. Alex runs fast. C; 3. The trees grow. A; 4. The Ender Dragon flies. B; 5. The squids swim. E

PAGE 24

1. ing; 2. ed; 3. ed; 4. ing; 5. ing

PAGE 25

1. wolves; 2. poppies; 3. churches; 4. husks; 5. days

PAGE 26

1. fast, Alex; 2. pink, pig; 3. hungry, horse; 4. scary, haunted house; 5. tall, Enderman

PAGE 27

1. so; 2. or; 3. so; 4. but; 5. and

PAGE 28

1. in; 2. on; 3. under; 4. on; 5. on

PAGE 29

1. Have you seen a shulker? 2. A shulker is a hostile mob. 3. It hides in its shell. 4. Its shell looks like a purpur block. 5. It opens its shell to peek outside.

PAGE 30

1. Steve is wearing diamond armor. 2. Creepers like to explode. 3. Ghasts live in the Nether. 4. Watch out for zombie villagers.

PAGE 31

1. C; 2. I; 3. I; 4. C; 5. I

PAGE 32

1. A zombie rides a chicken.
2. Baby zombies do not burn in sunlight.
3. Husks spawn from zombies.
4. A zombie attacked.

PAGE 33

Answers will vary.

PAGE 34

Answers will vary.

PAGE 35

Answers will vary.

PAGE 36

Answers will vary.

PAGE 37

1. F; 2. O; 3. O; 4. F; 5. O; 6. F; 7. F; 8. F

PAGE 38

Answers will vary.

PAGES 39–40

Answers will vary.

PAGE 41

1 – Feed the horse. 2 – Put a saddle on the horse. 3 – Ride the horse. 4 – Continue to feed the horse. 5 – The horse is tamed.

PAGE 42

1 – Collect two diamonds and a stick. 2 – Open the crafting table. 3 – Place the first diamond in the middle box of the first row. 4 – Place the second diamond in the middle box of the second row. 5 – Place the stick in the middle box of the third row.

PAGE 43

	fish	feather	leather	poppy
cow	X	X	O	X
chicken	X	O	X	X
polar bear	O	X	X	X
iron golem	X	X	X	O

PAGE 44

Answers will vary.

PAGE 45

Answers will vary.

PAGE 46

zombies / skeletons

fight back
stay away from cliffs
drop rotten flesh

hostile mob
undead
burn in the sun

run away when attacked
climb ladders
drop bones

PAGE 47

1. 2, 4, 6, 8, 10, 12, 14, 16, 18, 20, 22, 24, 26, 28; 28 legs

2. 5, 10, 15, 20, 25, 30, 35, 40, 45, 50; 50 blocks

PAGE 48

10, 20, 30, 40, 50, 60, 70, 80, 90, 100; 100 blocks

PAGE 49

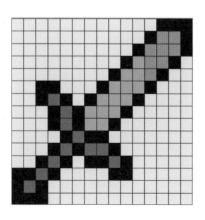

PAGE 50

1. 10, 12, 14; C; 2. 35, 30, 25; F; 3. 80, 90 100; A; 4. 4, 2, 0; E; 5. 80, 85, 90; B; 6. 21, 24, 27; D

PAGE 51

1. 17; 2. 19; 3. 19; 4. 17; 5. 16; 6. 18

PAGE 52

1. 18; 2. 17; 3. 19; 4. 15; 5. 11; 6. 13; 7. 14; 8. 12; 9. 16; 10. 10; 11. 8; 12. 20; Answer: It only learned to spell.

PAGE 53

1. 11; 2. 12; 3. 13; 4. 14; 5. 6; 6. 3

PAGE 54

1. 8; 2. 9; 3. 12; 4. 13; 5. 13; 6. 4; 7. 10; 8. 11; 9. 14; 10. 3; 11. 5; 12. 6; Answer: A bit of dumb luck.

PAGE 55

1. 11; 2. 11; 3. 15; 4. 8; 5. 7; 6. 9; 7. 17; 8. 5; 9. 9

PAGE 56

1. 9; 2. 9; 3. 14; 4. 5; 5. 13; 6. 13; 7. 9; 8. 3; 9. 10

PAGE 57

1. 19 books; 2. 9 books; 3. 19 items; 4. 8 books left

PAGE 58

1. 20 blocks; 2. 8 windows; 3. 6 emeralds; 4. 19 flower pots

PAGE 59

1. 3+7, 12; 2. 2+8, 16; 3. 4+6, 11; 4. 7+3, 10; 5. 5+5, 13; 6. 1+9, 18; 7. 8+2, 14; 8. 6+4, 19; 9. 5+5, 16; 10. 2+8, 18

PAGE 60

1. 9 + 9 = 18, 9 – 9 = 0;
2. 9 + 8 = 17, 9 – 8 = 1;
3. 9 + 7 = 16, 9 – 7 = 2;
4. 11 + 8 = 19; 11 – 8 = 3

PAGE 61

1	2	3	4	5	6	7	8	9	10
11	12	13	14	15	16	17	18	19	20
21	22	23	24	25	26	27	28	29	30
31	32	33	34	35	36	37	38	39	40
41	42	43	44	45	46	47	48	49	50
51	52	53	54	55	56	57	58	59	60
61	62	63	64	65	66	67	68	69	70
71	72	73	74	75	76	77	78	79	80
81	82	83	84	85	86	87	88	89	90
91	92	93	94	95	96	97	98	99	100

PAGE 62

1	2	3	4	5	6	7	8	9	10
11	12	13	14	15	16	17	18	19	20
21	22	23	24	25	26	27	28	29	30
31	32	33	34	35	36	37	38	39	40
41	42	43	44	45	46	47	48	49	50
51	52	53	54	55	56	57	58	59	60
61	62	63	64	65	66	67	68	69	70
71	72	73	74	75	76	77	78	79	80
81	82	83	84	85	86	87	88	89	90
91	92	93	94	95	96	97	98	99	100

PAGE 63

1. 4, 8, 48; 2. 7, 5, 75; 3. 6, 3, 63; 4. 5, 7, 57;
5. 7, 0, 70; 6. 9, 1, 91

PAGE 64

1. 30 + 8; 2. 80 + 2; 3. 40 + 4; 4. 50 + 3;
5. 60 + 7; 6. 10 + 9

PAGE 65

1. <; 2. <; 3. <; 4. =; 5. >; 6. >; 7. >; 8. <; 9. =;
10. >; 11. <; 12. <

PAGE 66

1. =; 2. <; 3. >; 4. <; 5. =; 6. >; 7. >; 8. >; 9. =;
10. =; 11. <; 12. >

PAGE 67

1. 67; 2. 88; 3. 71; 4. 49; 5. 88

PAGE 68

1. 37; 2. 88; 3. 96; 4. 48; 5. 58; 6. 43; 7. 93;
8. 85; 9. 55; 10. 34; 11. 78; 12. 73;
Answer: The streets are blocked.

PAGE 69

1. 31; 2. 41; 3. 43; 4. 43; 5. 22; 6. 34

PAGE 70

1. 34; 2. 32; 3. 43; 4. 31; 5. 62; 6. 41; 7. 22;
8. 33; 9. 54; Answer: It was a real blast!

PAGE 71

1. 12 heads; 2. 8 creepers; 3. 27 legs;
4. 15 eggs

PAGE 72

1. 21 diamonds; 2. 20 emeralds 3. 16 tin
ingots 4. 15 gold ingots

PAGE 73

1. 2 inches 2. 3 inches 3. 5 inches 4. 1 inch

PAGE 74

4. 3 inches 5. 4 inches 6. 5 inches 7. 2
inches

PAGE 75

1. 20 ounces; 2. 40 ounces; 3. 90 ounces;
4. 110 ounces

PAGE 76

1. 100° F, 38° C
2. 40° F, 5° C
3. 60° F, 15° C
4. 80° F, 27° C

PAGE 77

1. 9:15; 2. 7:40; 3. 8:20; 4. 2:15; 5. 4:35; 6. 6:05

PAGE 78

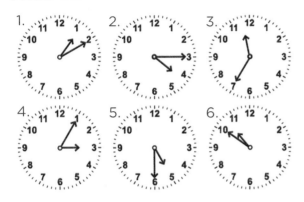

PAGE 79

1. 50 ¢
2. 58 ¢
3. 59 ¢
4. 82 ¢
5. 71 ¢
6. 62 ¢

PAGE 80

Answers will vary.

PAGE 81

1. C; 2. D; 3. A; 4. E; 5. B

PAGE 82

Monday: 20¢;
Tuesday: 60¢;
Wednesday: 40¢;
Thursday: 10¢;
Friday: 30¢

PAGE 83

Shape		Sides	Corners	Draw the Shape
triangle	△	3	3	answers will vary
rhombus	◇	4	4	answers will vary
rectangle	▭	4	4	answers will vary
circle	◯	0	0	answers will vary
square	□	4	4	answers will vary
hexagon	⬡	6	6	answers will vary
pentagon	⬠	5	5	answers will vary
octagon	⬡	8	8	answers will vary

PAGE 84

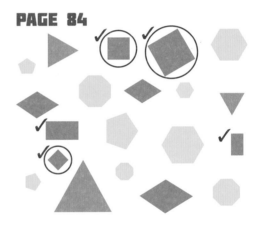

PAGE 85

1. triangle; 2. square; 3. rectangle; 4. hexagon

PAGE 86

1. cube, 6
2. rectangular prism, 6
3. cylinder, 2
4. triangular prism, 5

PAGE 87

1. 2 halves;
2. 2 halves;
3. 3 thirds;
4. 4 fourths

PAGE 88

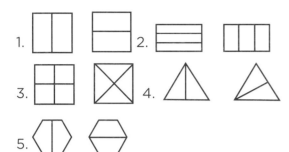

PAGE 89

1. N; 2. P; 3. P; 4. N; 5. P; 6. N; 7. N; 8. P

PAGE 90

1. wood; 2. fabric; 3. plastic; 4. glass; 5. metal; 6. metal; 7. fabric; 8. rubber; 9. wood

PAGE 91

Answers will vary.

PAGE 92

1. L; 2. S; 3. G; 4. S; 5. L; 6. L; 7. S; 8. S; 9. G

PAGE 93

1. yellow, hard; 2. brown; 3. white, sweet, light; 4. sticky, stringy; 5. green, smooth

PAGE 94

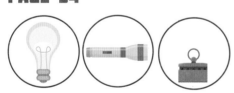

PAGE 95

Transparent	Translucent	Opaque

PAGE 96

1. T; 2. F; 3. F; 4. T

PAGE 97

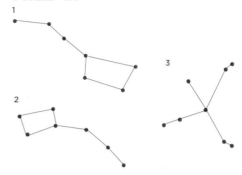

PAGE 98

New Moon

Waning Crescent

Waxing Crescent

Third Quarter

First Quarter

Waning Gibbous

Waxing Gibbous

Full Moon

PAGE 99

B	N	E	I	L	A	R	M	S	T	R	O	N	G	Z	U
U	Z	A	L	O	N	T	O	L	S	P	U	O	1	1	S
Z	U	A	P	O	L	L	O	1	1	A	E	P	S	P	F
Z	E	L	I	L	U	I	N	R	I	C	O	R	S	U	L
A	B	A	S	T	R	O	N	A	U	T	H	R	P	B	A
L	C	R	S	P	A	C	E	S	U	I	T	L	A	U	G
D	U	S	T	D	E	O	O	I	A	T	1	1	I	S	T
R	E	M	I	C	H	A	E	L	C	O	L	L	I	N	S
I	C	S	P	A	C	E	C	R	A	F	T	M	C	L	E
N	H	B	U	D	W	T	O	W	A	C	O	N	H	O	S

PAGE 100 AND 101

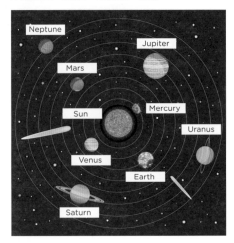

PAGE 102

T	E	M	O	U	N	T	A	I	N	S	E
J	P	L	A	N	T	S	N	R	W	U	L
U	A	U	M	O	O	N	O	W	A	N	I
N	S	R	O	C	E	A	N	S	T	U	S
G	E	T	I	D	E	S	L	K	E	R	L
L	R	L	G	I	O	V	J	Y	R	C	A
E	A	R	T	H	E	T	R	E	E	S	N
S	E	F	R	O	W	I	U	N	S	D	D
O	C	O	N	T	I	N	E	N	T	S	S
R	T	D	E	S	E	R	T	S	E	I	N

PAGE 103

Answers will vary.

PAGE 104

1. ice; 2. water; 3. water vapor; 4. water; 5. ice

PAGE 105

1. evaporation; 2. condensation; 3. precipitation

PAGE 106

1. energy
2. carbon dioxide
3. water

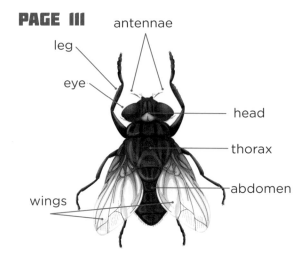

PAGE 107

1. C; 2. A; 3. D; 4. B

PAGE 108

1. T ; 2. T; 3. F; 4. T; 5. F

PAGE 109

First, an apple tree grows apples. Inside an apple are seeds. A seed becomes a sprout. The sprout becomes a sapling. The sapling grows into a tree.

PAGE 110

PAGE 111

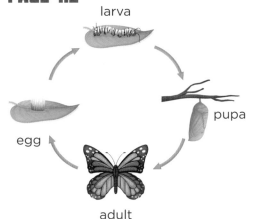

antennae
leg
eye
head
thorax
abdomen
wings

PAGE 112

larva
pupa
adult
egg

PAGE 113

Answers will vary.

PAGE 114

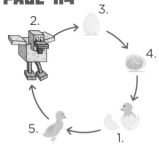

PAGE 115

Answers will vary.

PAGE 116

1. D; 2. C; 3. E; 4. B; 5. A

PAGE 117

Answers will vary.

PAGE 118

PAGE 119

1. B ; 2. D; 3. C ; 4. A

PAGE 120

Answers will vary.

PAGE 121

Answers will vary.

PAGE 122

✓ 1. obeying the rules
✓ 2. listening when someone is talking
✓ 4. cleaning up after yourself
✓ 9. looking for the good in others
✓ 10. saying you're sorry if you hurt
someone's feelings

PAGE 123

Answers will vary.

PAGE 124

1. T; 2. T; 3. T; 4. F; 5. T; 6. F; 7. F; 8. T

PAGE 125

Answers will vary.

PAGE 126

Answers will vary.

PAGE 127

1. B; 2. D; 3. C; 4. A

PAGE 128

M	A	L	R	O	P	D	W	A	S	R	K	E	R	A	L	L	T
F	A	T	H	E	R	O	F	O	U	R	C	O	U	N	T	R	Y
M	O	L	I	L	E	A	D	E	R	I	N	G	R	M	A	K	M
O	A	A	R	M	S	I	X	F	E	E	T	T	A	L	L	N	A
S	I	R	M	V	I	R	G	I	N	I	A	T	O	N	E	E	P
P	C	O	U	R	D	M	Y	F	A	T	I	S	E	P	R	E	M
A	R	M	Y	G	E	N	E	R	A	L	E	E	R	A	L	K	A
P	E	M	O	U	N	T	V	E	R	N	O	N	A	G	R	T	K
A	E	R	C	O	T	U	F	A	E	E	R	I	N	S	H	G	E
M	M	A	R	T	H	A	W	A	S	H	I	N	G	T	O	N	R

PAGE 129

1. president; 2. Civil; 3. slavery; 4. leader

PAGE 130

Susan B. Anthony worked hard to get women the right to vote.

PAGE 131

Answers will vary.

PAGE 132

Answers will vary.

PAGE 133

Answers will vary.

PAGE 134–135

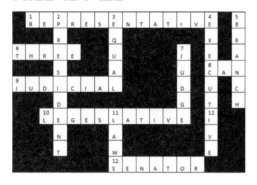

PAGE 136

1. C; 2. A; 3. E; 4. B; 5. D

PAGE 137

Answers will vary.

PAGE 138

1. 50; 2. Alaska and Hawaii; 3. Answers will vary. 4. Answers will vary. 5. Answers will vary. 6. Answers will vary.

PAGE 140

1. north; 2. west; 3. east; 4. south

PAGE 141

2. Answers will vary. 3. Canada; 4. Atlantic Ocean

PAGE 142

PAGE 144–145

1. Africa; 2. Europe; 3. Antarctica; 4. Asia; 5. North America; 6. South America; 7. Australia

PAGE 146–147

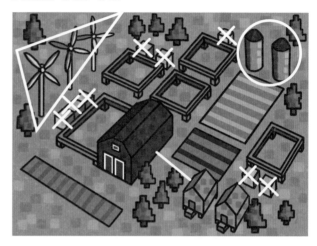

PAGE 148

1. D; 2. A; 3. E; 4. C; 5. B

PAGE 149

Answers will vary.